Unlock YOUR ability to create a life
of abundance and fulfilment
through the flow of energy

ENERGETICS EVERY DAY YOUR WAY

#1 Energy Coach

SUNAYANA CLARK

Energetics Every Day Your Way

First edition published and printed in the United Kingdom 2024

A CIP catalogue record of this book is available from the British Library.

ISBN (Hardcover): 978-1-0687078-0-3
ISBN (Paperback): 978-1-0687078-1-0
Imprint: Independently Published
Editor: Christine Beech
Typesetting: Matthew J Bird

For further information about this book, please contact the author at:
https://energeticseverydaywithsunayanaclark.co.uk/

Dedication

To my husband Jon and my son Charlie, my everything.

♥

Contents

Introduction   7

Part 1   13

Chapter 1: Why should we care about Energy?   15

Chapter 2: The Foundation   21

Chapter 3: Your Higher Self   29

Chapter 4: Deepen your relationship with your Higher Self   37

Chapter 5: Trust the Energy Flow   41

Part 2   55

Chapter 6: Your Higher Self and Manifesting   57

Chapter 7: Energetics Every Day and Your Health   71

Chapter 8: Energetics Every Day and Family   119

Chapter 9: Energetics Every Day and Money   145

My Love Letter to You   167

Acknowledgements   171

About the Author   173

INTRODUCTION

This book is aimed at two groups of people.

The first group consists of those who are curious. Those who believe there is more to this world than we can see. They are from many backgrounds - creative, faith-based or scientific; it does not matter. What is important, is that they are curious. It is this curiosity that has brought this book to their attention.

The second group that will be drawn to this book consists of those who are seeking change. They want to feel better about themselves, their health, their relationships and their finances.

If you fall into either or both camps, this book has been written with you in mind and is an invitation to explore the idea that more possibilities exist than you are aware of.

Energy is not mysterious or complicated. It exists, as we accept that gravity exists. In 1847, Hermann von Helmholtz stated in the Law of Conservation of Energy that energy cannot be created or destroyed. Einstein's formula of $E=MC^2$ recognises that energy can be changed into matter but it is not created to do so. It is the 'electricity' that exists in the space between particles and stops them from flying away. Sometimes it flows easily and quickly. At other times, it meanders and, sometimes, it hardly moves at all.

My goal, in writing this book, is to help you access this energy so that you can enjoy your life more. It will take practice and persistence, but this is a skill that, when mastered and used daily, will improve your life. You will experience more ease, more joy in your daily life, more peace and feel (and hopefully receive) more abundance in all forms.

Before I get into the details let me tell you a bit about myself. Ever since I can remember, I knew there was more to life than what is around us. It was a feeling, a knowing, but with no evidence to back it up.

Until 1977, when I was 9 years old and my dad took me to see Star Wars at the Empire Cinema in Leicester Square, London. I watched the film in awe and, when they talked about 'The Force', I remember feeling a huge burst of excitement. They were talking about what I knew existed and here was the evidence that someone else believed it too.

Fast forward to the mid-1990s, when I started my training as a holistic therapist and was introduced to Usui Reiki. Here was the magic I knew existed, in the form of therapy. I knew I could help people feel better with it. I became a Reiki Master Teacher in 1999 and aimed to teach the technique simply so that everyone could understand and practise it themselves.

For 21 years, I taught my students how to recognise the ebb and flow of Reiki, as they practised daily. I encouraged them to create an evidence log of their experience, as they noticed intuitive nudges and coincidences. This helped them to overcome scepticism and build trust in their practice, as well as to persist and remain curious.

In 2019, I met Olivia and Rafael Ocana who introduced me to my higher self, Athaliah. It was a revelation and opened up a new level of understanding that I hope to share in this book. Unbeknown to me, I had already been working with her when I was doing Reiki treatments, but now I could develop the relationship consciously.

As I developed my relationship with Athaliah, I began to do higher-self readings. She helped me take my clients through the energetic practices listed in this book. These are the basics that can change how you live your life.

For the religiously minded amongst my readers, this information could blend well with your religious traditions. I say this from a personal perspective, that your relationship with God is specific to you. It can be held within a vessel of religion but that loving relationship you have with Him is specific to you. Today, my relationship with God is more loving and truer than it has ever been. Please read this book with an open mind and allow yourself to ruminate on how it could fit within your personal relationship with God and His love.

For the scientists and the sceptics, I also ask you to approach this book with an open mind and a willingness to experiment. After all, is that not the essence of a scientist? To start with the hypothesis, gather evidence, and then analyse your results to prove or disprove the hypothesis.

I encourage you not to believe a word that I have written.

Yes, you read the above correctly.

Rather than accept everything I say mindlessly, I want you to play with energetics every day. Do not worry. It will not be onerous.

I want you to keep notes, track your goals and notice the following:

- Does my life feel better?
- What improvements can I see?
- Am I feeling calmer or happier?
- Am I experiencing more synchronicities or opportunities?

Form your conclusions and decide if using Energetics Every Day is useful. Might it help you live your physical life to the fullest?

Finally, why is this book called Energetics Every Day – Your Way?

It is because each of you is unique and will have lived life uniquely. You will have common experiences, such as going to school and playing games, but how you perceive and internalise those experiences will be unique to you. As you practise the exercises in this book, your perspective and experience of receiving and understanding will also be unique to you.

I do not want you to aspire to do this my way. I want you to learn how to work with your Higher Self and apply energy to your life in a way that is true to you.

My continuing wish is that when you learn this skill, it will bring you more joy, more fun, more ease, more appreciation, more, more, more of all that you want from this one physical life. In this energy of truth, you will gain the most from using Energetics Every Day.

We hope that you love this book as much as we have enjoyed writing it.

Love, always,

Sunayana, Athaliah and your Higher Self. x

PART 1

1

WHY SHOULD WE CARE ABOUT ENERGY?

Energy is the invisible glue that holds us all together and stops us from flying apart. It is the electricity between our atoms. It exists in every living thing on the planet, as well as running through, and around, all inanimate objects. It is the essence of nature.

We live in a physical world and our brain tells us what we are seeing. We choose to believe our brain because we can see, touch and feel the things it shows us. If you are curious about energy, the greatest challenge is that you cannot see it or touch it. You have to intuit it.

You may have experienced or heard of spiritual therapies such as Reiki, Rehanni, Theta Healing, Spiritual Healing or Spiritual Counselling. Some physical therapies, such as Shiatsu or Tui Na, also have a spiritual tradition. In these therapies, you experience energy flow. For the sceptics amongst you who regard these therapies as bunkum and believe what you can only see, touch or feel, then this book might be a revelation because of the skill that you will be taught and have the opportunity to practise for yourself.

But I promise you, you will not have experienced these energy practices. They will enhance what you work with already because you can combine them with everything.

If you accept the idea that everything started as energy, so before it became physical it had to exist as an idea, concept or feeling, then you should be able to accept the idea that, if you change the energy, you can change the physical outcome. That is the basis for this book.

Why should you bother with this?

You want to feel good. You want to love your life and squeeze every bit of enjoyment and experience from it.

If something in your physical world is not to your liking, you can, if you connect with the energy, interpret what you are feeling and begin to create a different reality. In my experience, that does not mean you get to transport yourself overnight to a new country or become a millionaire. Instead, through consistent action, you can bring about incremental change in a way that feels easy. The steps you need to take seem to just appear, or become clear, without having to be worked out. Life feels good and you are at peace, enjoying the flow and, even when things are not going to plan, you understand that if you stay in this place of trust, things will work out.

Change can happen quickly if you are truly aligned with what you are asking for, as long as there are no interfering doubts or beliefs. I have experienced amazingly fast change, which felt easy when the energy was aligned. For example, in 2021, I sold my house and bought another one, in 6 weeks, during the Pandemic. Everyone said it could not be done but I focused on who was going to buy the house, what we wanted in our new house and then looked at how the energy was flowing.

I will teach you how to do this.

I am not exaggerating when I say that this could potentially be the most life-changing book you ever read (assuming you put what I have written into practice).

Opinions

Everyone has an opinion about everything. If you choose to apply these practices, someone is bound to tell you that you are doing it wrong, that it is not the way, that it is the devil's work, or something else. Their opinion is formed from their experiences, their fears for you (they want you to be safe) and their love for you. For this reason, Sara Blakely, founder of SPANX, did not initially tell her family about her new business. When asked about it, she said, "When I first thought of SPANX, I didn't tell anybody for one year. Nobody told me not to share the idea with people. This was just a gut feeling that I had. After a year, I told my friends and family, and I heard, 'Honey, this is such a good idea. Why hasn't it already been done?"

When you follow other people's opinions of what you should or should not do, you give away your power. You are saying that your internal guidance is not good enough or does not work for you. You are looking for external validation.

When you start applying Energetics to your daily life, be cautious about who you tell. Hold it to yourself like the most valuable secret. While you build trust in your abilities and your Higher Self, you do not want other's opinions to derail you. This includes your mum, dad, siblings, best friend, Facebook friends, work colleagues, etc. After a while, you may begin to get compliments as people notice that you seem happier and they may ask what you are doing. You can then reply, "I'm choosing to focus on being happy."

When should you tell them? Perhaps never. I suggest you only talk about it when you know that your relationship with your Higher Self, and your faith in your ability to do Energetics Every Day to help solve your problems, are rock solid. If you do tell anyone, choose carefully who you do tell. You want them to be supportive not dismissive. For many years, I did not talk about what I could do with Reiki or what I have learned through working with Athaliah because I did not want to invite other people's scepticism or opinion.

Mind Monkeys

It is normal to feel anxious and nervous when trying something new.

My advice is to notice your mind monkeys but not engage with them. Instead, take action. Listen to the first audio recording or keep reading. Action and building a list of evidence will help you to overcome and quieten your mind. But, most of all, approach this with playful curiosity.

Mind Monkeys

What if it doesn't work for me?

What if I get it wrong.

What's the point?

I'm doing it wrong.

Treat this book like a workbook

When you are confident that you have understood the instructions in each chapter, practise them. Get comfortable with feeling unsure or even uncomfortable. There is no rush, or time limit, to move on to the next chapter and, when you feel the fear, remind yourself that, as you progress through the book, you are choosing a life of more ease and flow. There is a process for working with energy. There is a time to understand, a time to act, to pause, to understand again and then to take the next steps.

Keep a journal of your thoughts, understandings and progress. Note any questions you may have. Remember that this is not a race and there is no pressure to get to the end of the book.

What are energetic practices?

When you were a child, you probably used to daydream or make up stories as you played. By listening to an energetic practice, you can harness energy as you use your imagination. You can imagine the changes you are trying to create e.g. to remove a block or understand what course of action to take. You can supercharge this process by asking your Higher Self to connect to you and help you gain clarity and a new perspective, and to inspire you with the next step(s) you should take. The practices help to focus your imagination and tap into the surrounding energy.

Danger! Danger! Warning!

Applying the practices in this book will lead to a radical change in who you are and how you show up in the world. Are you ready to peel back the layers of hurt, judgement and experiences that have made you forget who you really are – a magnificent soul ready to shine and prosper in an abundance of friendship, love, money and opportunities, living life to the full with strong boundaries? You do not have to accept anything less than the best that life can offer you.

Having read this chapter, if you are ready to dive in, then let us start at the beginning.

2

THE FOUNDATION

Every single one of you has a Higher Self. If you are biologically male, then your Higher Self is male. If you are biologically female, then your Higher Self is female. You may have thought of them as your guardian angel. Their sole job is to help you with whatever you need assistance with. Most of the world's population does not connect consciously with their Higher Selves. Instead, they get a feeling or a sense of déjà vu. They may get a sense of 'I should call this person, or go there', but not know where that feeling is from. This is your Higher Self nudging you. These intuitive hits are general and random.

What if you could be more deliberate in your relationship with your Higher Self? What could you achieve?

This connection is the foundation of these practices. Your Higher Self can help you to flow the energy most easily, as well as improve communication. I will cover this later.

Who is my Higher Self?

Your Higher Self is the non-physical extension of you and helps you to translate your soul energy.

Their job is to help you live your life and fulfil your soul contract. In doing so, they evolve and grow, and their understanding adds to the Higher Self Collective. You are a unique soul for this lifetime but your Higher Self will have had many lifetimes, with other unique souls. When we refer to past lives, we are seeing our Higher Self's previous souls' past lives.

Your Higher Self has the knowledge and experience you need to accomplish what you came to do in this lifetime.

Your Higher Self is part of a larger collective of other Higher Selves. They can communicate and share information about what they are learning from you. This is how they evolve and grow. Depending on his or her path, your Higher Self may even have their own collective but, for the purposes of this book, I will not delve into this.

What is a Soul Contract?

Your soul contract is the framework which holds the agreements you made before you came to Planet Earth. How you would live your life, what you would experience and learn, and how you would evolve.

In this contract, you set out your milestone events, the 'what if?', 'what then?' possibilities, as well as who would collaborate in life with you. This includes your parents, siblings, partners, animal companions and culture, as well as your physical appearance. It also includes your abilities e.g. being musical, as well as potential careers, interests and hobbies.

Your contract was carefully curated over a long period to ensure your growth, as well as that of your Higher Self. It was created to help you evolve and learn how to connect to the perspective of love, understanding that 'Love is Assured for All'.

Your soul resides in an energetic tube (that will not appear in any X-ray) which runs from your pineal gland in the centre of the brain to the perineum in your groin. It is a beautiful energy that sees only the good and joy of life, the abundance of possibilities and choices that exist for us.

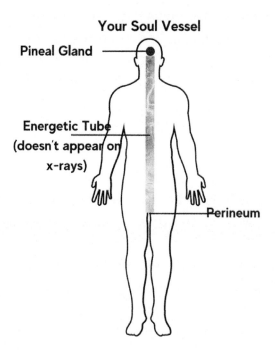

Your Soul Vessel

Pineal Gland

Energetic Tube
(doesn't appear on
x-rays)

Perineum

Is my whole life mapped out for me?

No, because you have free will, which is the ability to choose differently.

We do not consciously know, or remember, what is in our soul contracts. Sometimes we may feel boxed into a path or direction but, because we have free will, we can choose something completely different. Many people believe their lives are mapped out: they go to school, get a job, get married, have a family, and that is their life. For some, this feels great but others chafe against the path that they feel obliged to follow.

About ten years ago, the advent of the internet provided people with the possibility to become digital nomads. This new choice was in response to an energetic request for something different. For some of those people, becoming a digital nomad was NOT in their soul contract but they made a choice, based on free will and their circumstances, to do something different.

When we take advantage of our free will, our teams adapt to support us.

Another example would be to read this book and start your spiritual journey. You may have plenty of prompts or signs that you are being called to start but, because of free will, you can ignore them and carry on with your life. An allowance within your soul contract allows this to happen and your Higher Self will adapt if you choose to exercise your free will.

How does my Higher Self relate to my Soul Contract?

Your Higher Self helps you to live out your soul contract and will guide you when they can. As I stated previously, most people do not connect consciously with their Higher Selves, so the help that they can be given is limited. Once you start connecting consciously, you can make specific requests and they can then get to work on your behalf.

How will I know that I have connected with my Higher Self?

We each receive information differently.

- Some have a knowing; they just know what they know
- Some "see" amazing visuals which they realise are not from them, in their mind
- Others will hear the information as if someone is speaking to them
- A mixture of all the above

You also have the following vortexes of emotion (Chakras):

- Strength: near the perineum
- Truth: just above the belly button
- Hope: in your solar plexus (the 'unconscious gateway')
- Love: around your heart
- Trust: in your throat

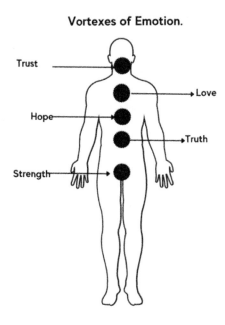

Vortexes of Emotion.

Trust

Love

Hope

Truth

Strength

As with many things, practice makes perfect. The more you connect with your Higher Self, the easier communication will be and the stronger your receiving will become. You may notice your Truth vortex is activated and have a strong sense that "this is correct or true". When you start, you may feel unsure and think you imagined it. Keep a note of what you receive and give yourself the benefit of the doubt. See what happens. Be curious, playful and open to what is unfolding for you.

How to connect with your Higher Self

Some of you like to read and others like to listen. Familiarise yourself with the process below and, if you prefer to listen as you practise the connection, please scan the QR code.

1. Find a quiet place where you will not be disturbed. Have a drink, a notebook and a pen to hand.

2. Close your eyes. In the centre of your brain, you have a gland called the Pineal Gland. It is the size of a green pea.

3. Visualise a tube running from the bottom of your pineal gland.

4. This tube runs through your brain, throat and into the middle of your chest. It continues through your digestive organs, past your belly button and into your pelvis, ending at the perineum in your groin. (Do not worry about being anatomically accurate. It will all be placed correctly.)

5. Imagine the tube now being filled with a beautiful white light, which is constantly moving and flowing. It might have flecks of silver, gold, pinks, blues, yellows or purples. Allow your imagination to take you through this vision. The tube looks as if it is bulging with energy and ready to burst. But, of course, that will not happen. The white light continues to move and swirl gently through the tube.

6. Ask your Higher Self to connect with you via the hope vortex in the middle of your diaphragm, where your solar plexus is located.

7. As he or she connects, invite them to weave their energy into your soul energy. This will help you feel the connection more easily. I imagine it as my Higher Self wrapping herself around my tube.

8. Ask your Higher Self to give you a clear sign that they have connected to you, by asking them to flow love to you. It might feel like a hug, a touch on your cheek, or a ticklish feeling. Some will experience a sensation, while others get

a feeling. When I first connected with Athaliah, I felt a stroking sensation on my cheek. Another friend had an itchy armpit.

And that is it. You are now consciously connected to your Higher Self. Yay! 😊

Sit in this space, learning to recognise your Higher Self's energy; and how they feel or appear to you. Ask questions and learn how you receive their answers. This is not difficult but it requires persistence.

Practise this daily until you feel comfortable connecting like this. It should not take long. Then you can ask your Higher Self to constantly stay connected and help you in all that you are involved in. Ask him or her to join you while you shop, cook, clean, have fun with friends and talk to your family. They would love to join you.

3

YOUR HIGHER SELF

In the previous chapter, I suggested that you invite your Higher Self to join you during your daily activities. When you do this, you can experience a beautiful flow throughout your day. By including them, you will build trust and a deeper connection. You will begin to know when you are being helped and what is being asked of you. Be curious and follow the nudge, intuition or feeling.

Two simple exercises which will help you build trust:

1. **Ask your Higher Self to help you cook a meal**

   This meal must be delicious and nutritious and take no more than 30 minutes to prepare. Your Higher Self can help you to eat better so when you have set the challenge, go into the kitchen, and see which cupboard you are led to open and what food you should take from the fridge.

   I do this a lot and I am always astonished at how delicious and simple the meal is. It is a brilliant way to retrain your taste buds, eat better and help your body receive the optimum nutrition it needs. At the same time, you are finessing your connection with your Higher Self. Depending upon what your body needs nutritionally, they may even get you to eat cake!

2. **Ask your Higher Self to be your GPS**

   You probably know all your local routes but, by asking your Higher Self to guide you, you can avoid traffic jams, road works and other obstacles. The way I do it is to ask if I should go left or right as I pull out of my driveway. Then is it left or right or straight ahead at the end of the road? You get the picture. Then one day, ignore every instruction and see how that journey unfolds. In my experience, I have run into more traffic or roadworks, and it always takes longer.

These two exercises will help you to believe that your Higher Self exists and wants to help you. It also builds trust in your ability to receive and interpret the guidance. Remember, there is no right or wrong to this; you are simply practising playful curiosity.

The Releasing Process

Once you are happy with your ability to receive and understand the guidance, you can ask your Higher Self to help you start to release the limiting beliefs or habits that are getting in the way of your enjoyment of life. This Releasing Process was first written about in *'Believe'* by Olivia and Raf Ocana (available on Amazon). Its purpose is to help you feel better and to have a more loving perspective about your life and your experiences. The point of doing Energetics Every Day is to feel good. By changing your perspective you are freeing yourself from: Guilt, blame, judgement, recrimination and so much more.

We all have habits and beliefs that keep us small or help us hide from feelings of unworthiness or feeling less than others, which may have developed from the following:

- An experience e.g. bullying

- A cultural memory e.g. persecution of a community

- A trauma e.g. the death of a loved one, including a pet

Our brains may not have processed these experiences and the feelings of horror, shock, fear, guilt or shame, which have been stored away, emitting a low vibration. Every time we experience some of the following emotions, more low vibration is generated:

Grief	Jealousy	Loathing
Hate	Anger	Sadness
Despair	Discouragement	Horror
Powerlessness	Rage	Guilt
Depression	Doubt	Worry
Frustration	Irritation	Impatience
Boredom	Pessimism	Overwhelm

Do you remember how I said at the beginning that everything is energy? Low vibration is just that. The energy filled with the above emotions is like clumps of sticky dark treacle in your body's energy matrix. If they are not removed, they will get embedded.

Eventually, that low vibration begins to influence your physical body. You may develop backache, tooth infection, regular headaches, colds, coughs, hives, irritable bowel syndrome, or something more serious such as diabetes, eczema or stiff joints leading to arthritic conditions.

High vibration can also be stored through the following emotions:

Happiness	Positive expectation	Hope
Excitement	Contentment	Optimism
Passion	Empowerment	Joy
Freedom	Appreciation	Gratitude

Thanks to our Higher Selves, we can feel better when we remove the low vibrational energy clumps through the following Releasing Process:

1. Connect to your Higher Self.

2. Ask to be shown a memory, or a group of memories, connected to a feeling e.g. shame, and the very first time you felt this. This is the source or primary event which still triggers you. Then, each time you felt shame, the original experience was built on. By addressing the primary event, the subsequent events can be cleared.

   Please note, that you are NOT re-experiencing this memory. You are replaying it.

   This is not about blaming anyone. You are an objective watcher of a memory. Notice them but do not give them any thought. You are preparing to remove these memories so that they no longer trouble you.

3. Ask your Higher Self to show you a new perspective and help you create a new truth about a memory e.g. feeling shame when scolded as a young child, the new truth might be: The Truth is that God loves me.

   Why would that be true? Because in that moment of shame, the low vibration clump made you forget how loved you are by God. It made you feel separate and alone.

One word of warning: the Releasing Process can be exhausting. Therefore, you must prioritise rest, sleep, hydration (drink plenty of water), good nutrition and being in nature. You might be disinterested in things you usually like, but this will be temporary. It is because you need to conserve energy and your Higher Self is helping you through the changes.

Do not do what I did which was to complain a lot. Instead, accept that the physical discomfort is temporary and will pass.

What is a Truth?

It is an energetic resetting of your beliefs, based in love (instead of fear) and agreed upon with your soul. A new Truth is full of lightness and has high vibrational energy. It clears out memories associated with shame and helps you to energetically forget them. You may struggle at times to align with the truth but that is okay. You are going through an adjustment of thought and perspective. If you do struggle amend the Truth statement to say: "The Truth is I desire to.." By saying I desire, we are signalling that we are getting ready for change. Again, be patient with yourself and, if needed, ask your Higher Self to explain why this is the truth.

Some memories you revisit might involve family members and you may feel cross or upset. This process is not about casting blame. They did what they could with the knowledge they had at that time. If you get caught up in the emotions of anger or blame, allow them to be expressed, then apply the Releasing Process.

In addition to releasing the low vibration you have stored; you can let go of your Transitional Vibration.

Transitional vibration is the energy (feelings) you generate daily. This happens from the moment you open your eyes to when you go to sleep. A funny conversation will generate a high transitional vibration. A scary or sad experience will generate a low transitional vibration. Mid-transitional vibration is generated by familiar experiences and evokes little or no response, as they feel neither good nor bad.

The media you consume can greatly affect your transitional vibration e.g. the news and violent programmes can create low vibration (your brain cannot distinguish between real and fictional violence, or nearby and distant violence) whilst sports events, comedy nights and uplifting programmes or podcasts can generate high vibration.

This morning, I sat with my husband in a comfortable loving silence. It gave me great satisfaction since our friendship and love was palpable. This was a high transitional vibration generation moment.

If you do not process and release this daily transitional vibration, it is stored in your physical cells. Before you go to sleep each night, review your day and find things to be thankful for. Replay the funny conversations and the things that made you feel good.

It will help balance your transitional vibration, especially if you have had a stressful day.

Be patient with yourself and allow this process to unfold. Trust that your Higher Self knows what he/she is doing.

Keep a note of all the truths that you create so that you can revisit them throughout the process. It can take some time to get through, but it will be worth it when you notice that you feel happier, and life does not seem as hard as it once did.

By the end of the process, you will notice how your perspective has changed. You will find it easier to reframe a challenging circumstance into a more positive one. You will realise that YOU are in control of your thoughts, beliefs and actions.

This is powerful and is the starting point for the change you want to experience in your life.

When I went through the Releasing Process, I had a notebook filled with truths and a note on my phone where I added them daily. When I needed to reinforce my new beliefs, they were written on Post-it Notes where I could see them regularly.

Your Higher Self can guide you through this process efficiently and in the most loving way. Trust them and let them help you. You will not have to revisit every low-vibration experience. Sometimes, lots of memories will be swept up together as you clear a main memory. As you do this, you will help yourself to change in a simple but effective way.

The Releasing Process

Your guide to releasing low stored vibration with the help of your Higher Self.

Step 1.	Step 2:	Step 3:	Step 4
You find yourself triggered and are experiencing a strong emotion.	Your Higher Self reminds you of a past experience that is still triggering you today.	Your Higher Self will give you the Truths you need to release these emotions and memories.	Repeat this process noticing how much happier you are gradually feeling. Your Higher Self will tell you when you have completed the process..

4

Deepen your relationship with your Higher Self

By now, if you have implemented the previous chapters, you will be experiencing a beautiful daily flow with your Higher Self and hopefully beginning feel more optimistic.

You know that you can trust your Higher Self and want to get to know them better. It is time to ask them more questions.

Take your time with these questions. Some answers may not flow easily, or you may be uncertain about what you receive. If so, ask your Higher Self to confirm their answer and bring it to you as easily as possible – that is part of their job.

I have left space below for you to write the answers if you wish. Take your time with this, as some answers may not land for a day or two.

1. What is your name?

2. What is your favourite song?

3. Do you have a favourite colour or image I can associate with you?

4. Do you have a special skill that you help me with?

5. Show me a capability I do not know about (this is an energetic talent which can be artistic, healing, manifesting, bringing ease or joy to others, or an interest in a specific subject).

6. Tell me about one of your previous souls. What do we have in common?

7. What did we do for fun in the non-physical?

8. What can we do for fun here on Earth?

9. Why did you want me to be your next soul?

10. How can I help you?

Your relationship with your Higher Self is based on equality. He/she is your non-physical best friend, so you want to have fun together, remember how you were non-physical together and know how you can help each other.

Keep asking questions. What other things would you like to know?

5
TRUST THE ENERGY FLOW

Your Higher Self will function as your guide as you feel into the energy flow through the exercises in the next chapters. This is why you have been given your Higher Self so that you can collaborate easily and optimise your results.

Energy flows constantly but this flow can be affected by our beliefs and desires, and our willingness to follow the nudges. Each of you will understand the energy flow in the easiest way for you. Some will feel the flow, some will know how it is flowing and others will receive visuals. It does not matter which way you receive it, as long as you allow yourself to. Over time, you may find that this expands to include other ways.

1. Connect with your Higher Self.

2. Set the intention to feel the energy flow around you.

3. Imagine seeing a golden flow of energy going out from you and connecting with the energy around you. It may flow from your forehead, heart, solar plexus or tummy.

4. How does it feel? What do you notice? Does it feel sluggish or free? Heavy or light? Wide or narrow? Is there a block or bottleneck? Trust the way you receive it, as this is not something you can get wrong.

That is it. Practise feeling the flow with different things, such as the following:

- Think about a route you will take. Does the flow of traffic feel easy or congested?

- Think about a school or work assignment. Is the flow moving freely, getting stuck or meandering? Practically, if stuck or meandering, you might have been struggling to complete the assignment.

- If you have a website: how does the energy of it feel? Full of life or invisible? This is the window to your business and you want it to be visible.

- If you have a manifesting target e.g. buying tickets for a sold-out concert: how does the energy feel? Full of possibilities or shutdown.

- If you have argued with someone and want to understand how to make up, feel the energy flow before you act.

There is no limit to what you can feel into. Feeling the flow will help you gain understanding and find your starting point. Once you know the starting point, and the outcome you seek, you can apply Spiritual Intention Protocols (SIPs).

If you intend to send a boost of energy to your website or the sale of a property or car, check your thoughts. Fear indicates that you need to release and create new Truths. These thoughts could include 'No one wants what I am selling', 'What if I get cheated?' or 'I won't get paid what my services, property or car are worth' or it is not safe for me to be visible or seen

However, if you feel expectant or excited at the thought of boosting the energy of your website, you will radiate a high vibration. This is the place you want to start. Eventually, you will notice that you almost always radiate at a high vibrational starting point.

Keep a note of how the energy flow feels. There is no right or wrong feeling. Once you can perceive your starting point and the energy flow, it may be time to apply a Spiritual Intention Protocol (SIP).

Spiritual Intention Protocols (SIPs)

These are instructions to the energy which can speed it up, clarify, magnetise, release the flow, slow it down and much more.

In 2021, my house was up for sale. We had a short deadline because the stamp duty reduction would end in six weeks and our buyers and sellers were nervous, we would miss the deadline. We were waiting for the surveyor to get in touch and had been told it could take up to two weeks. This felt really frustrating and worrisome.

I connected with the energy flow between me and the surveyor and it felt slow and sluggish. I was guided by Athaliah, my Higher Self, to use the SIP "Energise' Within thirty minutes, I received a call from the surveyor and explained our problem regarding the deadline. He told me he could not come any sooner but that the information would be with our bank and the solicitors within 24 hours. I reassured our buyers and sellers and advised the solicitor. Sure enough, we completed our sale by the deadline. The SIP had sped up the energy flow, which allowed the necessary information to become available. As a result, I could feel good about the process.

That is the beauty of SIPs.

There are many SIPs, and your Higher Self can help you to use the correct one to aid your energy flow.

Using SIPs

1. Connect to your Higher Self.

2. Think about your desire.

3. Notice how the energy flow to this desire feels.

4. Ask your Higher Self to help you choose the relevant SIP.

Common SIPs

Energise	Clear	Clarify
Magnetise	Flow	Allow
Release	Free	Rearrange
Dissolve	Manifest	See
	Accept	

Your Higher Self may suggest others to you. There is no limit to what you can do to help yourself achieve your goals or desires by following the energy flow and using the SIPs at appropriate times.

- Get a new job or promotion at work

- Choose where to go on holiday

- Manifest money

- Find a partner or improve a relationship

- Improve your journey to work

- Improve communication

Accomplish a goal or desire

Here are more examples of when I have used SIPs, having understood the energy flow, whilst travelling:

I was travelling into Central London when it was announced that the Tube I was on was delayed due to a signalling problem. We would be delayed by at least thirty minutes while the repair teams figured out the problem. I would have been late for my appointment, so I connected to Athaliah and asked to be shown the energy flow. I could "see" that the flow was disrupted by a switch which was an easy fix. I asked Athaliah to share the problem and the solution with the Higher Selves of the engineering repair team. We used the SIP 'See' and, less than ten minutes later, we were on our way.

Recently, I had another experience on the Tube. I was shown that the signals were creaky and old. I asked for the SIP and was given 'Grease' so I asked for the signals to be energetically greased with energetic WD40. As a result, my journey was uneventful and I arrived home easily.

Spiritual Intention Protocols are powerful when used with the Truths you create with your Higher Self, as you work through your Releasing Process and beyond. These Truths are aligned energetically to the truest version of you. When combined with SIPs the outcome will be turbo-charged.

Perhaps you have never got on with your older sibling and they have always been hostile. By connecting to your Higher Self, you can begin to understand their point of view. Perhaps they are experiencing the 'Oldest Child' wound when a sibling is born and the oldest child wonders, "Was I not enough?" They may feel unworthy of their parents' love and constantly try to prove their worth.

As a result, you may have fallen into practised roles of behaviour. Either aggressor/victim or muting yourself so that they will never feel outshone or overshadowed. You could, with help from your Higher Self, create new truths, such as:

- The Truth is that I did nothing wrong when I was born
- The Truth is that we are both loved by our parents and by God
- The Truth is that it is not my responsibility to make my sibling feel better

Once you have created all the Truths needed, you can ask for a SIP to help everyone e.g. 'Dissolve'. The intention here is to dissolve any old behaviours that maintain hostility and get in the way of making peace.

Once that has taken effect, you may receive a nudge or feel the energy flow to use another SIP to rebuild the relationship.

Unexpected Consequences

When we ask for change, through a desire to feel good or restore balance, the Energetic Universe goes to work on our behalf. However, more factors than we are aware of need to be arranged to allow our manifestation to occur – there are eight billion people on the planet all asking for their desires too. Sometimes, there can be unexpected consequences of asking for change using Energetics.

Recently, I was due to fly to India to help my mum with the sale of our family home. Three days before I was due to fly, I got a message to say the sale had been held up and I needed to postpone my journey. I was not thrilled as I had already rearranged work commitments. I am human and do not like changing my plans at short notice. However, when I felt the flow of energy, I felt the rightness of the delay and begrudgingly changed my ticket.

Within a couple of days though, the cause of the delay became clear. There was a bureaucratic hiccup with the sale and the buyer had to leave town unexpectedly, due to a bereavement. This delayed the sale by fourteen days. On the positive side, I saw my son come home from university, so my husband would have company and help to manage the house when I later left. Also, the temperature dropped from the mid-40s Celsius to a more comfortable 30s, after some rain.

Unexpected consequences are not to be feared. At the time, you might feel astonished, irritated or shocked but you will quickly understand the reason.

Trust and Allow the Flow

We like to know the 'How?' e.g. How will my desire come? We often want to know the whole route which can, in reality, be overwhelming. The 'How?' is a thought we generate because we like to feel in control. When we work with our Higher Selves, we do not need to know everything from every angle because we trust that we will not be let down. This is why it is important to build a relationship because we operate from our hearts rather than our minds. Rather than focussing on the 'How?', we should be noticing the nudges and direction of energy flow.

The writing of this book is a beautiful example of trusting and allowing the flow. I had written about 80% within eight weeks and began to wonder how I was going to publish it. Many companies charge a lot of money, as much as £8000.

I decided to ask Athaliah what I should do. The first thing she showed me was a landing page on my website, with my book for sale. She then showed me my book, available to purchase from Amazon in paperback and on Kindle. I was also shown the flow of sales for my book.

This gave me a direction and I knew I had to create a landing page and format the book for self-publishing on Amazon, and as an e-book.

When I asked Athaliah, "How do I go about self-publishing?", I kept hearing the name of a friend who I had not spoken to for a few years. When I looked her up on social media, imagine my surprise when I discovered she had retrained as a book coach.

I sent her a message explaining my situation and, at her request, booked a call. That one-hour call taught me many things I needed to know about self-publishing. More importantly, she generously shared contacts for an editor and typesetter, both of whom have helped to develop this book. Thank you, Sarah, Christine and Matt.

If it was not for Athaliah showing me the energy flow and the actions to take, I would have spent a lot of time fretting about publishing, researching online, feeling daunted by the cost and may never have published this book. I would have expended mental energy trying to figure out the why, what, when and how.

Instead, I have met lovely helpful people, feel confident in my methodology and have an affordable and easy-to-follow plan of action. I do not need to worry about the 'how?' This book is being written and published with a feeling of ease.

This is such a powerful gift as a result of trusting the energy flow. It will never steer you in the wrong direction. Trust that, even if you do not have the whole picture, what is unfolding will always be the best outcome for you.

Time Management

When you follow the energy flow and the nudges from your Higher Self, you will prevent a lot of wasted time and be more efficient in your day-to-day activities.

Practical exercise:

On a piece of paper, list four things you have to do today. You may be unsure which order to do them in the time frame available.

Connect to your Higher Self and ask to be shown the energy flow and the order in which your jobs are to be done efficiently.

Some of you will feel the flow by looking at your list and seeing the first job jump out at you. Others will need to close their eyes and use their imagination to see which one is first, second and so on.

Number the jobs. That is your action list for today and, if you follow that flow, you will get them done in the most time-efficient way.

As you feel into the flow, you may realise that energy is not flowing to one of the jobs. Ask your Higher Self, "Does this job need to get done today?" or "Should I do it another day?" You should feel a clear answer. If another day, ask, "Which day?"

The Importance of Asking Questions

This is your ONE physical life to live. Yes, your Higher Self and the energy know where you want to go and what you want to achieve or experience, and they can guide you. But, if you do not understand or agree with the guidance, then what?

Ask questions.

Earlier, I suggested that you ask your Higher Self questions to get to know them better, as this builds trust in the relationship. In the same way, you need to ask questions for clarity of what is being asked of you.

Simple questions include:

- I do not understand what you are trying to convey, please show me another way.

- Why are you showing me this?

- What is the next easiest step for me to take?

- Please explain why the energy is flowing this way.

- What will happen if I choose not to take this action?

- Is there an easier alternative approach?

- Is this True and Important for me?

The final question is a powerful one to ask when you are unsure about deciding. "If I do this, will it align with the Truth of Me; to my Inner Being or soul desires?" I ask this frequently and I find that, as soon as I get the answer, my energy settles and I stop waffling over the decision.

In February 2022, some friends invited a group of us to stay for the weekend of 25th June 2022. I love being with these amazing women, so it felt like a no-brainer to say yes. Except, when I asked, "Is it True and Important for me to go?", I got a 'No'.

I was astonished and periodically asked again but kept getting the same answer. In the end, I declined. I would not have known then that on 25th June 2022 I would be with my mother-in-law as she passed away due to cancer. When the original invitation was extended, we did not know that she was ill.

Asking if something is True and Important also demonstrates trust in the energy. It will not steer you wrong.

Positive Overwhelm

This is when there is an accumulation of energy in your physical body. It can make you feel:

- Miserable and even weepy.
- Discombobulated or dizzy.
- Exhausted.
- Doubtful of your Higher Self and whether this is all real.

Ironically, it is called 'positive' overwhelm, when it feels the opposite.

Take a deep breath in and out, and say, "Let Out." This will help you restart the energy flow.

If you are experiencing Positive Overwhelm, it is important to get enough sleep, go outside in nature (hug a tree, if you can), rest and eat well.

The Power of One

I cannot emphasise the impact and influence that you have as an individual. You may feel insignificant when it comes to world events, but you can make a positive difference to your family, friends, colleagues and local community by how you show up.

We have probably all been impacted by negative people and made to feel miserable.

Everything is energy and, when we interact with others, our energy ripples out and meets other ripples. That is how influence and impact are felt.

Having gone through the Releasing Process, your vibration will have risen and, hopefully, you feel happier. Your family, friends, colleagues, and those you interact with, may have begun to notice and comment.

If you want them to feel good, you can impact them positively by deciding how to show up with your Higher Self, e.g. with an anxious relative, you may wish to show up with an energy of ease or 'everything is achievable'. Simply asking that the best version of you shows up in all interactions can have an impact on those around you and you will also feel better for being that person.

To do this, connect with your Higher Self and say how you want to show up. That is it. It is so simple, but I promise it is effective.

My friend, Louise, flows with ease all the time so everything I do with her feels easy. I notice the difference when she is not with me.

Try it and notice your feelings and the reactions of those around you.

PART 2

6

YOUR HIGHER SELF AND MANIFESTING

Manifesting is the idea that, through the power of belief, we can effectively 'think' a goal into reality. It is a form of magical thinking as we believe that our hopes and desires can influence how the world unfolds. This concept has been around for centuries but has gained renewed interest in recent years, especially due to popular books like *'The Secret'* by Rhonda Byrne.

It means having a desire and deciding that you want to experience it, e.g. you may want to hike to the base camp of Mount Everest. The outcome and feelings you experience are the manifestation.

Some people believe that it is 'mind over matter' but, in my experience, what is more powerful is the combination of understanding the energy, clearing limiting beliefs, and then taking action. When manifesting with your Higher Self, you make sure that the energy is clear (because if you change the energy, the physical experience will change) and take aligned action steps.

Most people's desires revolve around three areas:

- **Health**: physical appearance, longevity, flexibility, as well as mental and emotional fitness.

- **Wealth**: streams of income and financial freedom.
- **Love**: all relationships including animal companions and love for self.

Within these are the material desires you want to experience e.g. holidays, running marathons, owning your own house, etc. Living life to the full, not inhibited by your health, with beautiful fulfilling relationships with family, lovers, colleagues and friends.

How can your Higher Self help?

Your Higher Self can flow nudges, ideas and inspiration but you have to choose to act, as this is YOUR ONE LIFE. Some manifestations will come to you without much effort. But others, the ones you are hung up on and dream about repeatedly, may need more consistent action and faith over a longer period. The signs and nudges are the language of your Higher Self. It's how they communicate with you – allow yourself to have these conversations.

Manifesting for Others

Your desires should be about YOU experiencing good things. Often, we want manifestations to enhance someone else's experience, but that is not always helpful.

Suppose you see a friend experiencing financial hardship and you want to win some money to help them. This desire is borne out of a caring and compassionate place. However, it does not consider what your friend can learn from that experience e.g. how to manage their finances better. They may be disempowered if you give them money.

I am not saying that you should never help but make your desires for you and let others take care of their desires. You may feel that this is selfish or unkind but remember the linear viewpoint. You do not know what will come out of this experience for your friend.

By asking your Higher Self how you can help and understanding the answer (and energy flow), you may find a better way to help that empowers your friend more e.g. introduction to a specialist or mentor, or information about a job opportunity.

When you successfully manifest for yourself, you demonstrate to others that it is possible for them. You can have an impact and influence your friends and family and, if they are ready for those changes, they can start their journey. This refers to the Power of One that I mentioned in the previous chapter.

When you manifest for yourself, you are responsible for your journey and no one else's, including your kids. This produces strong boundaries and loving relationships. If I won the lottery jackpot, I would not give my son all the money he wants because it would deprive him of opportunities and experiences of work.

What might those opportunities or experiences be? He could meet a mentor who will help in his career or his life partner at work. As part of his soul contract, he could build a successful business. But if I pay for everything, so he does not have to work, he will miss out on those opportunities or experiences.

It is not that I will never help him, but I would do it carefully so that he still has a purpose and can experience his life to the full.

How can you Experience Manifestations?

Set your desire: What do you want to experience? A trip? More money? Better relationships? Better health? A new car? The limit to your desires is only what you set.

I need to add a caveat here.

As you deepen your understanding, make sure that your manifestation is something you truly desire. You should light up on the inside when you think about it, and it will make you smile.

As a beginner at manifesting, start small with something that has little or no emotional impact but will help build your trust and exercise your abilities.

- Spot the yellow car: these are uncommon but, when I am in the car with my family, we see them all the time.

- Abraham Hicks (of Law of Attraction fame) used butterflies to ramp up trust and exercise ability. Set your desire to see them wherever you go, no matter the season. Wait and see what happens. They will start showing up on TV, on posters, in jewellery, fluttering around you, and oh so many other ways.

Take action: As you begin and use the above examples, you will probably have no deep-seated beliefs about yellow cars or butterflies. But, as you progress and decide on more personal manifestations, you may encounter the following worries.

- Your inability to achieve your goal or desire.

- Your worthiness to achieve your goal or desire.

Do you need to do some releasing around these limiting beliefs? What must you do to keep your vibration high with each step? A simple action could be to contact a specialist travel agent for an initial conversation.

Before you take any action, you must feel good about your desire and the prospective step. If you want to go on a trip, feeling excited before talking to the travel agent is the perfect energy needed to make the call.

After the call, the costs may cause you to worry that you will not have enough money to pay for the trip. Take time to steady your thoughts and feelings before the next step. This might be to set a savings goal. Remember to only act when you feel good (or excited) about the next step.

Celebrate the outcome: Each time you complete an action step, take time to savour how you feel. Manifesting is as much about feeling good as it is about experiencing all this life has to offer. There is no limit to what you can desire or achieve, other than your own beliefs, feelings and actions. Keep repeating this process until your desire has manifested:

Set your desire + Take action + Celebrate the outcome

My friend and communication coach, Beth Turner, says: "Marry the process, divorce the outcome." Your job is to stay focused on your desire and to take action.

For many people, the reason they do not get their manifestation is because they focus on the lack of what they desire i.e. they have not got enough money or have not met the person of their dreams or I want it immediately. This is human nature. Impatience kills the momentum and feeds frustration.

Remember that you have the power to change your mind and choose differently. The Universe is filled with energy that responds to your feelings, not your words or thoughts. I will cover this later.

You need to recognise your starting point. In other words, how are you feeling about your desire? Does it seem like an impossible dream? If so, you are showing low vibration.

Your work is to know that you are worthy of your desires and can experience them all.

Example: While writing this book, I was aware of a repetitive thought: what if people think I am mad or do not like what I have written? My vulnerability indicated that I had to work on feeling safe, so to resolve this:

1. I spoke to Athaliah for reassurance.

2. I felt the flow of the book which was loving and expansive, and I felt the information was needed.

3. I asked, "Is this book true and important?" and the answer I received was a resounding "Yes!"

The support I received from Athaliah and the knowledge that this book was needed gave me the confidence to continue writing and commit to publishing it.

Another example might be if you are sending energy to your website, you may fear public opinion or a negative response and wonder if people will buy your product. These are indicators that you need to release limiting beliefs and low vibrations and then create new Truths. But if you feel expectant and excited about your website's energy, you will start from a high vibrational stance which will make it easier to manifest.

How can your Higher Self help you?

Some desires are linked to your soul growth and will propel you forward, but others are physical human desires. Your Higher Self can help you with manifestation by flowing nudges, ideas or inspiration but you have to choose to act because this is your ONE physical life. Some manifestations will come to you easily but the ones that you dream about repeatedly may need consistent action over a longer period. This is due to your vibration and degree of allowing which is why you have to keep choosing.

You see things linearly but your Higher Self has an overview and can show you which step to take and when. Using the previous example of wanting to go on a trip, they can help you find the right travel agent who will help you achieve your desire with ease.

1. Set your desire.

2. Connect with your Higher Self (by now, that connection should be almost automatic and you will trust that you are connected).

3. Talk about your desire. Why you want what you want and how it will make your life better. Let your Higher Self feel your hope, excitement and joy at the thought of achieving your desire.

4. Ask them for the first step you should take. Do you need to release any beliefs? Is there someone you need to contact? Is there something you need to do?

5. Make sure you feel good before acting.

6. Take the first step.

7. Allow any emotions to settle before repeating this process.

Alignment + Action = Powerful manifesting

When you first practise this process, it can feel slow and frustrating. Stay aligned with your desire, keep feeling good and be alert to your thoughts. Are they highly vibrational or demonstrating a scarcity mindset?

Scarcity mindset v Abundant mindset

A scarcity mindset is rooted in lack and fear. It believes that there is not enough money to go around and that there are no good men or women. It believes that the world is 'going to hell in a handbag' and can find no reason to be optimistic.

You will know someone like this. They complain all the time. They fear that jobs are being stolen and that anyone different is dangerous. They pity the young for not being able to get on the housing ladder whilst criticising them for being entitled. They delight in talking about all that is wrong. Much of the media and many politicians demonstrate scarcity mindsets. They are unpleasant to be around and, if you are sensitive to energy, you will quickly feel exhausted by them because they negatively impact your vibration.

When you want to manifest something that you desperately want, to make your life better, you must first choose to change this scarcity mindset.

Changing your Scarcity Mindset

Notice your thoughts, especially the cyclical ones. An example could be that you want a new car. Why you want it does not matter, it is enough that you want it. Every time you think this thought, your next thought might be "I do not know how I can afford it" followed by "Everything is so expensive" and "I do not know how anyone can afford anything, as the cost of living is so high". This is a scarcity mindset and this cyclical thought pattern will repeat on a loop whenever you think about purchasing a new car. You may wish to also create a new Truth such as "I live in an Abundant universe" or "the Truth is everything is working out for me".

Some cycles have a trigger thought which immediately triggers the next thought, then the next, and so on. This cycle becomes practised quickly and, when you are dealing with a scarcity mindset, you must notice it and action a change. As soon as you notice the thought, think of someone you love. It will break the cycle easily.

You will have other repetitive thoughts, around various subjects, which feed the fear of scarcity. However, as you release your limiting beliefs, you will find it easier to notice them and stop the cycles.

Abundant Mindset

An abundant mindset sees possibility and opportunity. It is rooted in love and can see and feel hope, love and trust. Individuals with an abundant mindset know that, in the face of adversity, they can find a solution (hope). They trust their abilities or know someone they can turn to, and they are often great to be around as they lift you. They are encouraging and share their wisdom.

An abundant mindset knows that there is more than enough to go around and wants to share. They believe that everything will work out and that they will be okay in the end. People with abundant mindsets make you smile. They give you a sense of being accepted and recognised for who you are and value you for being you.

As you begin to adopt an abundant mindset, start noticing nature. Nature is full of abundance of colour, variety and form. When you walk around, count how many shades of green you can see. You will be astonished. Nature always shows us abundance. We just have to notice.

The Process of Manifesting

This process is simple to understand but harder to implement. Be willing to work with your Higher Self, improving the connection. Why do things the hard way, when they can help you manifest more easily?

Set your desire, knowing that just because you want your desire or that experience it is enough.

How do I truly feel about my life? Is it great or am I feeling a lack of money or love or something else?

1. Ask your Higher Self to help you receive a new perspective and make peace with where you are right now

2. Notice any cyclical repeating thoughts and stop them.

3. Start appreciating the good things in your life and feel gratitude.

4. Allow yourself to receive inspiration

5. Act on that inspiration, even if it makes no sense.

6. Hold your high vibration steady while you wait for your manifestation.

7. Allow yourself to receive your manifestation.

Repeat steps 2- 6, refining your connection each time, releasing any more limiting beliefs, improving your understanding of your inspirations, and getting better at acting on those inspirations. Every time you do this, you will improve and increase your allowing.

Then choose it again - and again - and again. You have to be willing to keep choosing this process until you get what you desire.

What did you notice in the process?

Manifesting is not a passive process

Read that sentence again. YOU are totally in charge of this process of refinement.

- YOU decide YOUR wants.

- YOU RELEASE YOUR limiting beliefs.
- YOU CHOOSE to do this consciously.
- YOU CHOOSE to believe.
- YOU ALLOW and ACT on the inspiration received.
- YOU RECEIVE.

I write about 'allowing' in the steps above. It means making peace with where you are now so that you can open the gate to let in what you are asking for.

It is the act of surrender i.e. I am where I am. It is not where I want to be but that is okay. I know that I can trust that what I am looking for is also making its way to me.

It is difficult to allow when you are in a state of resistance i.e. grumbling or moaning about how hard life is, how unhappy you are or asking when the manifestation will come to you. It is important to allow yourself to make peace with where you are before any of the changes you want come to you.

In your choosing, you say that you are worthy of all you desire. You are going to allow yourself the opportunity to receive all that you desire. You are willing to make the necessary changes to become the person who can receive the manifestation. This is the secret: your worthiness.

You have to be the person who is ready to receive what you desire. Therefore, be prepared to grow, learn and change. Be curious, patient and playful and be confident that you will get what you desire. It just might not show up as you think it will.

The following chapters focus on health, relationships and wealth and how working with your Higher Self can help to create the changes you desire.

Be patient

We live in a world where time is important and we are taught that it is part of being courteous and thoughtful. There is a right time to do things, but the Universe does not move in the same timeframe. It has millions of moving parts to be synchronised for your manifestation to occur, most of which you know nothing of.

Therefore, do not fret that your manifestation has yet to arrive. Instead, concentrate on the only thing that is real, the present. Tomorrow is yet to come and will be influenced by today. Focus on keeping your vibration high, finding joy and ease in all that you do today. Focus on your allowing and keep choosing the life you want. That is your work. Leave the rest up to God and the Universe, who have your back. I promise.

Summary

Manifesting is the idea that, through the power of belief, we can effectively think a goal into becoming reality.

Focus on manifesting your desires. You may want to help others but let them find their solutions.

Alignment + Action = Powerful Manifesting.

Scarcity mindset v Abundant mindset.

The Process of Manifesting:

- Set your desire.
- Release any limiting beliefs.
- Notice your thoughts and feelings.
- Allow yourself to receive inspiration.
- Be patient and stay in a place of knowing that your desires are coming to you.
- Allow yourself to receive your manifestation.
- Keep repeating the process until the manifestation arrives.

Manifesting is not a passive process.

Be patient.

7

ENERGETICS EVERY DAY AND YOUR HEALTH

*W*ARNING: *Energetics can be used alongside conventional medications. Please continue to take prescribed medication as there may be severe unforeseen consequences if stopped.*

So far, you have connected to your Higher Self and learned how to understand the flow of energy and what might interrupt or hinder it. You have also learned that you manifest with the help of your higher self and the flow of energy.

Energetics can help in many other ways. As with everything, practice makes perfect. Keep a journal of the nudges or understandings you have so that you can track your journey.

Opinions

As previously stated in Chapter 1, everyone has an opinion about everything. Other people's views can kill your excitement and hope. Your desire for change may ignite fear in the person you tell, and then you will need to expend energy supporting them, which will distract you from your goals. Their fears are none of your business.

Continue to work with health professionals and combine this with your energetic practice. As this supports conventional medicine, there is no need to mention it.

Health

The holistic model of health covers emotional, mental and physical aspects, which are intertwined and related.

Emotional health is energy. As the basis of your health and GPS, it is an effective way to know if you are on the right track. Your health reflects your connection to the planet, spiritual life and communities. A lack of ease (or dis-ease) causes disconnection and translates into illness.

Transitional Vibration and Stored Vibration

In Chapter 3, transitional vibration was described as the energy (or feelings) you generate throughout your day – either low, mid or high.

If this is not processed and released, it becomes stored vibration in your physical cells.

How can Energetics help?

When diagnosed with an illness, you are being called to understand and let go of the disconnection and fear you have experienced. Healing is found by accepting who you are and what you have experienced, and then letting go of the emotional charge of those painful events. They have been sitting in your energetic body as low stored vibration and contributing to unconscious behaviours you have used to feel safe or loved.

Because they remain unprocessed, the affect the physical body creating illness.

By working with your Higher Self through the Releasing Process, you can let go of this perspective and love your physical body with compassion and a new appreciation.

Examples of how illness can form in the physical body:

Your body is amazing. It works constantly to keep you in a state of balance (homeostasis). When things go wrong, it indicates a problem through minor irritations or illnesses. If these go untreated vibrationally, they may develop into something more serious.

Stress is one of the biggest contributors to disease. It places pressure on all the body's systems, disrupting appetite and the ability to sleep well or feel happy. When stressed physiologically, high cortisol levels are experienced which trigger the Fight, Flight, Freeze or Fawn responses.

Energetics also affect **genetics** which can be cultural as well as familial. If you grew up in a former Eastern Bloc country you may remember living in a controlled environment with little individuality, since the former Soviet Union clamped down on personal freedoms and creativity. Those memories may be triggered energetically if you later find yourself in a controlling relationship, resulting in low vibration being stored.

Your **lifestyle and beliefs** will reflect your feelings. You might believe you are unwanted because of what you experienced growing up. You may expect people to reject you. On the surface you have lots of friends, but no close friends who know you well, since you try to protect yourself from potential rejection and hurt. You may have poor boundaries because you are seeking external approval. You may struggle to get promotions or build a successful business.

How does stress lead to illness or disease?

Low vibration can be described as continuous stress which can generate feelings of sadness, helplessness, loss or unworthiness. When we do not process these heavy emotions and let go of the fear, we store them as low vibrations.

You may fear being alone, feel unsafe and disconnected from God or unworthy of His love. I appreciate talking about God may repel some of you, so use a term that you feel more comfortable with e.g. Source of Life, Universe or science.

When difficult emotions are processed healthily you can find a new perspective, based on love. Not a romantic love, but one that is unconditional, non-judgemental, uplifting and ever-present. I would characterise that as God's love.

How can an experience develop into an illness?

Illness is the physical manifestation of low vibration which comes from repeatedly experiencing emotions of sadness, grief, loss, unworthiness, lack, guilt, jealousy, hate or anger.

For example, you may have been bereaved at a young age. Your brain and physical cells have learned about shock, grief, loneliness, loss, anger, and even jealousy of those who did not experience that early on. As you grow older, you may experience more bereavement in friendships, pet animals or redundancy.

If these feelings are not processed, they will build up, layer on layer, into sticky dark treacle-like low vibration. Gradually, this pattern of belief begins to have an effect. It may start simply as a bad mood you cannot shake off. You become critical or annoyed at simple things and overreact. It starts to show in your thoughts and behaviour. You become pessimistic, not wanting to plan. "What is the point?" you ask. "It all goes away in the end." When my Dad died, I refused to plan more than a month ahead because there was no point. Today I do not have that resistance and am happier to plan for the future.

You pull away from friends and family and keep your guard up so no one can get to know you. You think they will not accept you as you are, and you cannot rely on anyone to stay. This reinforces your feelings of loneliness, separation and jealousy.

LOW VIBRATIONS & ILL HEALTH.

Trauma

Shock, Anger, Grief, Jealousy, sadness, rage experienced.

Layering the original feelings.

LIfe events occur

Time

Niggling Health Problems begin to occur

Stuck in a cycle of trying to feel better but nothing sticks.

Physically & mentally Exhausted, feeling hopeless.

More serious illness diagnosed.

75

You may seek comfort through online games or Netflix in the safety and comfort of your home, where you do not have to talk to anyone or see others having a good time. You may even develop a gaming or food addiction but, although these behaviours bring a modicum of comfort, the good feeling will not last.

You get stuck in a cycle of trying to feel better whilst maintaining separation to protect yourself from feeling lost and lonely. This starts with a feeling of hope, then disappointment as there is no improvement, then hurt due to loneliness, then anger or jealousy, until you are back to feeling lost, sad and lonely. Thus, the layers keep building.

Eventually, it becomes so practised that you no longer notice the cycle. It becomes entrenched and is your new reality.

Feeling lost & lonely.

Hope (that you can make friends).

Withdraws

Nothing really changes

Feels rejected

Anger/Jealousy

Feel disappointed.

No improvement in making friends

You may notice small irritating health problems e.g. a more frequent tummy ache or a disruption to your sleeping pattern.

These will eventually normalise but, as time goes on, you develop more serious issues e.g. blood pressure problems or diabetes.

In Louise Hay's book, *'You Can Heal Your Life'* she says that diabetes is "longing for what might have been. A great need for control. Deep sorrow. No sweetness left."

To halt this, you must reverse your behaviours and beliefs and begin to influence your genetics energetically. In the holistic world, this is called 'breaking inter-generational patterns'.

Let me tell you a personal story of the effects of stress and emotions.

Thirteen years ago, my dad died unexpectedly and it led to a falling out with his family over his property. This generated feelings of loss, grief, sadness, anger and judgement.

About four years ago, I developed a lump in my chest which became infected and needed two rounds of antibiotics to clear it. It reappeared and I went to a breast clinic where the consultant said it was a lipoma (cyst filled with fat) and was of no concern. It remained in the centre of my chest, almost over my heart.

Fast forward to earlier this year and the property at the centre of the row was sold. Within two weeks, I noticed that the lump began to change. Within a week, it was a full-blown carbuncle (boil) in the centre of my chest, and it was red and painful. I decided to treat it energetically and with hot compresses but set a deadline that, if no better within four days, I would make an appointment to see my GP.

Story to be continued ...

How can Energetics improve your health?

Previously, I posited the theory that everything is energy and, if you change this, you can change the physical manifestation, which includes mental and emotional problems.

DO NOT stop taking any prescribed medication without speaking to your doctor.

We are seeking a shift in perspective from fear to love. Fear encompasses the many low-vibration emotions mentioned above. Whereas, love suggests feeling calm, hopeful, curious, peaceful, cheerful, productive, happy, joyful, and having a positive outlook with excitement and anticipation.

So how do we start?

With a desire for something different.

You may not know what different will look like. It might be "I just want to feel less sad" or "I want to feel calm". That is enough. It is this thought that will help you to start making changes as it gives you a direction.

Pursuing this feeling is not a straight line. Initially, you may only feel less sad for 5 - 10 minutes before familiar thoughts intrude and the practised thought cycles start again. With time, it might be for half a day or a full day. If you persist, you may feel less sad but also experience moments of peace, or occasionally, hope. Eventually, those moments of peace and hope become longer and in time become your dominant feeling.

Our feelings function as a sat nav and can guide us to a higher love-based vibration.

In 2019, I decided to stop worrying about the future. I wanted to feel that everything would work out for me. Each morning, for 13 months, I listened to a 15-minute audio called *'Everything is Working Out for Me'* by Abraham Hicks on *YouTube*.

Did I believe it in the beginning?

No, but as I listened, I began to look for signs of things working out for me e.g. an unexpected client booking, the solution to paying a bill or getting the information I needed easily. I noticed that I was feeling less stressed when I thought about the future. In fact, I was feeling more optimistic.

This translated into feeling that I could make plans for future events. I started with insignificant things and built up to more important plans for my business or involving my family.

An initial feeling led to a simple action, which led to a change in behaviour, which led to more trust, and then to an even better feeling, more actions and different behaviours to now, when I know everything will work out for me.

I do not need to know every step of the journey. This has freed me and I only need to know and believe everything will work out. By changing my beliefs, I have created a new self-fulfilling experience.

Practically, I will always recommend that you connect with your Higher Self and do the Releasing Process (see Chapter 3) but that might feel too hard for you currently. Connecting to your Higher Self is the quickest way to change your vibration because he or she will show you what needs to change, but if you cannot do that, ask yourself:

What is the simplest thing I can do, right now, to feel better?

- Play music
- Listen to an inspirational speaker
- Send a message to someone
- Go in the garden
- Tidy your desk
- Fold your laundry
- Cook your favourite meal
- Pot up a plant
- Recite your favourite prayer
- Sing
- Dance

It does not matter what you do. Just do the simplest, easiest thing. When that is done, you will feel better, comforted, or relieved. Then you will begin to create high transitional vibrations.

Once that first task is completed, ask yourself again:

What is the simplest thing I can do, right now, to feel better?

It might be to take a nap or have a bath. Do it and accumulate more good feelings. Make sure you document your journey.

This question also applies if you are at work, as there is always something you can do to feel better. You will be surprised at how quickly it becomes a habit, and then you will be ready to build on it by connecting to your Higher Self and doing the Releasing Process.

Remember that this might take time, which is okay. There is no rush. You are just committed to feeling better. It is that simple. It took about thirteen months for me to develop a solid unwavering belief that everything will work out.

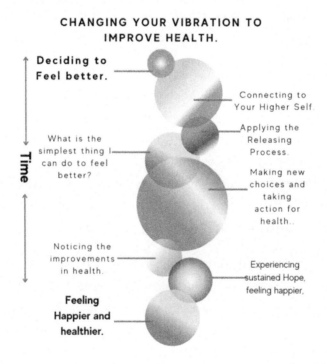

CHANGING YOUR VIBRATION TO IMPROVE HEALTH.

Deciding to Feel better.

Connecting to Your Higher Self.

Applying the Releasing Process.

What is the simplest thing I can do to feel better?

Time

Making new choices and taking action for health.

Noticing the improvements in health.

Experiencing sustained Hope, feeling happier,

Feeling Happier and healthier.

I hear you asking, "But, Sunayana, how does that help with my illness?"

As you choose to feel better, you will gradually change your habits without even noticing. You may also feel strong enough to go through the Releasing Process. Old habits will lose their allure as you choose to spend your time differently.

You might join a local walking group or find people with common interests. You might start a class or accept new opportunities. As you choose what makes you feel happier, life will become sweeter. You will replace old beliefs and patterns of behaviour with new ones.

This combination with the Releasing Process, which alters the energy (feeling), is powerful and will lead to changes in your behaviour. As we know, (say it with me) when the energy changes, the physical manifestation must also change.

It is important to manage your expectations. I do not promise that you will wake up tomorrow with your illness healed. I am showing you a road map of how to change the energy behind it and gradually change the manifestation of the disease. The time this will take depends on how well you let go of the past and choose high vibrational emotions. Changing beliefs and habits requires commitment. Start each day by connecting with your Higher Self and asking for help to actively choose to feel better.

Physically, you will start to see signs that you are on the right path. For example, if you have diabetes type 2, your sugar levels may begin to stabilise. You will make better food choices, perhaps starting a new eating regime to prevent sugar spikes. This may lead to weight loss or lower blood pressure. Eventually, your medical practitioner may agree that you have improved significantly enough to come off your medication and be considered free of diabetes. This process could significantly improve your diabetes within 3 - 6 months, but you must consistently apply Energetics and be prepared to do the inner work.

Back to the story of my carbuncle ...

By connecting with Athaliah, I gained insight into the beliefs I held about my family's treatment of me. These included the unfairness of the situation, loss of relationships with my extended family, and a sense of being a victim and martyr. I had also taken responsibility which was not mine to shoulder alone.

I understood that:

- everyone was doing their best in the situation
- everyone was hurting and reacting from that place of hurt

The two truths that brought the most relief were:

- The Truth is that I am not responsible for everyone's well-being and I release this burden
- The Truth is that I accept them (my family members) as they are, with no requirement to change

These were important because they helped me create boundaries and experience freedom. The last truth made me realise that, while I had felt judged, I had also judged my family members harshly. By accepting them and not asking them to change, I could accept that they were divinely loved, as I was, and deserving of forgiveness. Through forgiveness, I could let go of all the pent-up emotions and energies.

Four days after I started the Energetics and hot compresses, the carbuncle popped. I instantly felt better and did not need antibiotics.

By trusting my Higher Self and the Releasing Process, I was able to release those strong emotions held in my body. If I had not let them go, the result would have been worse. Athaliah showed me that they were negatively impacting my body's ability to regulate itself.

The other thing to note is that I surrendered to the process of healing with Athaliah. I did not question or worry about the path I had chosen. All my attention was focused on healing my limiting beliefs, letting go of those feelings that had festered, and changing the physical manifestation of the problem – the carbuncle. I was focused on feeling better, which is the outcome we are always seeking when using Energetics. In that surrender came an allowing that I no longer needed to be that judgmental angry person and that I was worthy of good health. I was also free of all the low vibrational cognitive thought cycles and able to choose to think differently about my extended family. It also helped me to trust my body more. Each night, I spend a few minutes sending loving thoughts and flowing love to my cells.

I encourage you to keep talking and listening to your body.

Trauma related to Anxiety and Depression

Trauma is defined by the UK charity Mind, as "a stressful and frightening experience, or a distressing event which is out of your control. It could be one incident or an ongoing event over a long period."

This can include abuse, bullying, bereavement (including pets), an accident, brain injury, as well as experiencing, or witnessing, something shocking.

Your brain is wired for survival. When you experience a traumatic event, it can leave you in a sensitive or triggered state i.e. your brain remains hypervigilant for danger.

How can Energetics help with Trauma?

Energetically, a traumatic experience triggers beliefs, such as:

- I am unsafe

- I am unworthy

- I am alone

- I am unlovable

- No one will help me

- There is no one to rescue me

Physiologically, a traumatic experience triggers the vagus nerve. This is the longest nerve in the body and is responsible for telling the body to increase levels of the stress hormones, cortisol and adrenalin. Since the brain and physical cells are exposed to high levels of these, over time they get used to the pattern of stress and trauma.

You may experience sleep disruption or a constant urge to eat or drink. Cravings for high-fat and high-sugar foods are common, as well as feeling exhausted all the time. You feel unsafe and, for some, that may translate as a need to hide. You may become hypervigilant about your surroundings.

This can become your normality, but it is not normal or how you should experience life. By using Energetics, you want to be calmer, more in control and feel better physically. Remember, changing the Energetics also changes the physical experience.

Sometimes it feels easier to apply the physical changes first e.g. take vitamins, sleep more or improve your diet. You may repeatedly try to change things physically but, whilst your beliefs remain the same, it is hard to make a sustainable long-term change. I hear some of you say, "But how have people managed to deal with their trauma and related symptoms?" It is because they got used to feeling sad or unsafe, and developed other behaviours to help them feel safe.

But the signs are evident that something is not right and they may develop anxiety. Others develop OCD, eating disorders or other psychological disorders. Relationships can be strained because there is a trust issue, or they have problems with money, boundaries or deadlines. These are all visible symptoms of an unprocessed trauma but the person is so used to them that they have forgotten that they are due to an experience when they felt unsafe.

They have not forgotten the experience but cannot connect it to their behaviour. Coping habits and mechanisms only work so far because their brain remains on high alert.

If you have experienced trauma, listen to this energetic practice to release and forget the memory and the attached beliefs.

You can listen to this audio here

"Releasing Traumatic Memories"

Once you begin to do this, it is important to soothe your body. Depending on the cause of the trauma, you may choose to exercise or allow yourself to be pampered. For some, refusing social invitations will be soothing, others may need talking therapy to recover or creative outlets e.g. writing or movement.

Remember to be gentle with yourself. Prioritise sleep, nutritious healthy whole foods, and gentle exercise.

Energetics and Anxiety

Anxiety is a normal response to a dangerous situation. However, trauma-related anxiety is an abnormal response to a normal situation e.g. meeting friends. It can become a well-honed response and quickly become a pattern.

The brain needs to be desensitised so that it starts to recognise everyday situations as normal so that dangerous situations can be identified more accurately.

Using energetics, we can:

- understand the impact of the trauma
- see a wider view of the trauma
- perhaps understand if this was a soul-contracted event and then create new truths that could lead to a more loving perspective.

This perspective helps us to release the low stored vibration thus deactivating the effects of the traumatic event. This breaks the cycle of being triggered and storing more low vibration.

When I work with anxious clients and we understand how the trauma plays out in their lives, we then look for simple behaviours that bring comfort. I like to get my clients to do something that reminds them of better times and feel connected e.g. cook their favourite childhood food, as there is comfort in those meals which remind them of time spent with mothers or grandmothers. One client cooked kneidel soup with her mum from scratch and said it gave them respite from the anxiety they felt about her mental health. Baking cakes and going to the park reminds me of a lovely childhood with my mum. A jar of pickled red chillis in oil, sitting on a 1970s-style gas fire, will forever be associated with my paternal grandmother who lived with us when I was a child.

Which childhood activities evoke a feeling of comfort in you?

Keep a note of them and, as you work through releasing your trauma, try these activities.

Disease and Conventional Medicine

I am based in the UK where we have a brilliant healthcare system called the National Health Service. It is staffed by people who are deeply caring and skilled at their jobs. Conventional medicine is a fantastic way of getting a diagnosis and understanding what you are facing. After all, knowledge is power. Many medicines and surgical techniques are essential, excellent and serve a purpose e.g. if you find a lump, you will stop the problem from getting worse by having a lumpectomy. Even though you have not changed the Energetics or made any lifestyle changes, that does not mean you should allow the lump to grow. Sometimes, swift physical intervention is necessary.

Your doctor may prescribe conventional medication, which can work alongside Energetics.

Energetics can give a new perspective to find ease with your diagnosis. From a place of ease, you can approach related decisions in a calmer frame of mind.

First, feeling into the energy of your diagnosis can be used to find a better feeling about it. We can understand what has contributed to the diagnosis i.e. the source of the low vibration and its associated emotions.

A recent client has had a painful swollen ankle since 2020. She had gone down the NHS route and the rheumatology consultant had administered a steroid injection which made little difference to her ankle but gave uncomfortable side effects.

In our 90-minute session, I could feel there was a lot of fear, judgement and shame associated with her ankle, which was caused by childhood experiences and relationships. Through discussion, we found new truths she could align with and this created a change in the vibration. By the time we ended the session, my client reported that her ankle was moving better. Within 48 hours, it was almost pain-free. That is how fast the change can be!

Energetics can be used to:

- communicate with medical professionals and enhance their work

- maximise the benefits of the medication and minimise side effects

- nutritionally support our bodies through treatment

There is so much we can do with Energetics to support conventional treatment, by being at ease with the experience and clearing any fear generated by the treatment.

Energetics and Cancer

A cancer diagnosis fills people with dread. The treatment protocol is physically harsh and mentally exhausting, and the side effects can be extremely uncomfortable. Hair loss and skin irritation are additional burdens to bear. For many, the prognosis makes them feel unsafe and life can feel uncertain.

The shock effect also needs to be considered e.g. finding a lump and the diagnosis. Speedy treatment can improve survival rates but leaves little time to process the diagnosis and what is to come.

In sharing the news, you may also have to deal with the shock and upset of those you tell, as they will have their triggers around illness and death. I spent the first thirteen years of my career as a holistic therapist working as a volunteer or paid therapist for various cancer charities and know that it is an extremely unsettling and scary time for the patient and their family and friends.

Two things struck me during that time.

- Cancer rarely appears out of nowhere. The body often shows signs of dysfunction e.g. an inability to shake off a cold/cough, followed by something more serious e.g. pre-diabetes or blood pressure problems over about two years.

- After the gruelling treatment regime, when officially in recovery, it was common for patients to develop depression or anxiety. This was related to the diagnosis and speed of the treatment, which had not allowed them time to process or accept what was happening.

How can Energetics help?

Energetics (and your Higher Self) can bring:

- Ease with the diagnosis, treatment and side effects

- Understanding of active beliefs and patterns of thought that have contributed. e.g. what is eating away at you?

- Comfort by reducing the sense of helplessness that your body has let you down or fear of your mortality

Your connection to your Higher Self will help you understand the cause of the cancer and the events and beliefs which led to the diagnosis. For example, do you have a belief that cancer runs in your family? What events led to this diagnosis and what perspective shift is required? Armed with this information, and releasing these beliefs, your attention can be focused on the treatment so that you can be at ease before it starts.

Once you identify your trauma or stress event (it may be a culmination of several events), you can use the Releasing Process with your Higher Self to reframe those memories. When I worked in cancer charities, the trauma experienced by patients was often caused by divorce, bereavement, children leaving home redundancy or a change in employment status.

You can ask your Higher Self for help to improve your diet which will support your body during treatment. You can be helped to ask better questions of your oncologist, surgeons and nurses.

They can help you get the rest you need. Since you are doing this with an energy of Ease, you will approach this challenge differently than from a state of shock and stress.

How to find a place of ease

By working with your Higher Self to understand the cause of the cancer and what needs to be released, you will have a sense of control. Your Higher Self can also help with the food you should eat during treatment, and when you should rest and go out into nature.

You must prepare your physical cells by working in concert with them and talking about medical procedures and medicines, and how they can choose to react. Reassure them of your love and flow this to them. Imagine your heart overflowing with love for every cell in your body and letting it seep through to each of them until they bask in this love. Let them know that they can cope with all that will happen and that they can heal.

With the help of your Higher Self, unconditional love can be sent to the medical personnel involved in your care. This will shift their low transitional vibration (remember the tube journey I mentioned) and help them be better at their jobs.

If you are taking any medication, ask your Higher Self to flow unconditional love to this, to minimise the side effects and maximise the efficacy.

I have seen this in action with a dear friend of mine. I am in awe of how she navigated her year of cancer treatments with such ease and how well her body reacted and continues to react. She lost her hair but was not exhausted or in much pain. Her surgeon and oncologist have both remarked on how well she has recovered.

At the beginning of this chapter, there was a reminder to keep taking your medications. Use Energetics to improve their efficacy and then, in consultation with your medical practitioner, wean off them as appropriate. You don't have to choose between conventional medicine and energetics because they work beautifully together.

Place the medication between your two palms. Connect with your Higher Self and bless the hands that made this medication, bless the doctors, nurses, oncologists, porters, pharmacists and medical secretaries, as well as the bus or train driver who will get you to the hospital - anyone involved in your cancer journey. You will not know many of them, but they will be involved.

Focus your intention on the medication and ask that the efficacy will improve, with minimal side effects. Do this with each new prescription. You can also apply this process to IV medicine by staring at the medicine and asking your Higher Self to help you flow a blessing. This is essentially love, which always beats fear.

Weight

PLEASE NOTE: I am not a nutritionist and do not advocate specific meal plans. Check with your medical practitioner before any changes in your diet especially if you are on medication.

If you have a medical condition, continue to take your medication and have your regular health checks. Using Energetics will combine easily with this and you will see the benefits.

Weight is an emotive subject. We are pushed and pulled by social media, traditional media, cultural norms, and our feelings about our physical bodies. When your weight fluctuates, your body responds to your feelings. So, the first thing, we want you to do is to accept where you are.

You may consider yourself too thin or too fat. That is okay because today is the first day that you are going to begin thinking differently about your body. Instead of being focused on the outer appearance you are going to begin to believe that your body is amazing. It is that simple. It performs so many functions without you even thinking about it: breathing, temperature regulation, hormone production, repairs and more. The weight fluctuations indicate that something is off-kilter energetically

Can you accept that?

If you can, it is a good place to start. Now, you can decide if you want to create a change or are happy to maintain the status quo.

You may not be ready for change. That is okay. Perhaps finding ease in where you are is the most important aim because that will generate the least transitional vibration. With that ease, you may be able to drink more water or choose to eat more nourishing food. That would be a good place to be.

Your soul contract contains your physical characteristics i.e. height and weight, as well as the colour of your skin, eyes, hair, etc. It is all there. Possibilities are allowed for, depending upon what you experience as a physical human. These are called 'What if, if then' outcomes.

What affects weight?

Feelings + beliefs + habits = weight change

No one is born overweight or underweight. You were born beautifully perfect but life's experiences can leave you feeling vulnerable, unloved, without control or 'less than' compared to others. This can leave you feeling disconnected from God.

These experiences create the limiting beliefs mentioned previously and you may want to become invisible, hide or feel happier. They lead to habits that support the feeling e.g. over-eating or not exercising.

What is happening vibrationally? These feelings are stored within the physical body, in your cells, as low-stored vibrations. They can lead to habits that support your feelings and beliefs but do not support your weight.

Therefore, to change your weight you must:

1. Address your feelings.
2. Use the Releasing Process to change your beliefs from a fear-based perspective to a loving one. Aim to release your core belief that allows you to accept that God never abandoned you and that you are safe. He loves you and can be trusted.
3. Adopt habits that support your new feelings and beliefs.
4. Embrace the wonder of your body, as it is utterly amazing.

The process is:

1. Connecting with your Higher Self.

2. Ask to see the experiences that led to your feelings.

3. Use the Releasing Process to let go of the emotions you have been holding onto. The experiences may be nuanced and layered, so be patient with yourself.

4. Ask for help to change your habits. Your Higher Self will know the most effective way to do this e.g. to change eating habits or move more.

It is important to change your habits and rewire neural pathways.

It is that simple but, when it comes to health, it takes time to notice a physical difference and it doesn't always feel easy

Let us dive into this a bit deeper.

Some people gain weight whilst others become anorexic or bulimic. The following table shows common experiences that lead to weight changes but it is not an exhaustive list.

Cause	Feelings Evoked	Belief
Emotional or physical abandonment	Scared Alone Fearful of the unknown Resisting change	I am not safe No one will help me I am alone
Abuse	Scared Filled with horror	I am unlovable I am disposable

		I am unworthy of love
		It is my fault
Neglect	Scared / Sad / Lost / Pessimistic	I am unworthy of love
Comparison	Rejected / Not good enough / Misunderstood	I am unworthy
Bereavement	Experiencing loss / Alone / Abandoned / Angry / Sad	No one will rescue me / I am alone / No one else will love me as they did
Change	Uncertain / Unsure / Anxious	I am unsafe / I am in danger / No one will help me

These six causes are over-arching themes which can contribute to weight gain or loss. I have seen, amongst my friends, that when they have felt unsafe, food-controlling habits take over. I have experienced this as well.

I had an unconscious eating habit which led to a huge weight gain. I was using food to feel happier i.e. looking for the dopamine hit. It was caused by unresolved feelings from my childhood and, once they were resolved, I was able to change that habit.

It is important to change the habit because, by choosing differently, we can consciously rewrite the neural patterns.

My ongoing weight loss journey has consistently evolved since I started working with Athaliah. Before that, I had tried most of the well-known slimming clubs, and the latest fad diets including meal replacements, and exercised regularly - Pilates, HIT classes, walking and belly dancing, to name a few.

Nothing worked in the long term. I would lose a few pounds and then it would come back. Through the Releasing Process, I had to come to terms with some experiences that I had avoided and forgive myself for them. I blamed myself, but Athaliah showed me a new perspective. I was a vulnerable child and the adults could have done a better job of looking after me. I was shown that they did their best with the knowledge they had then. It did not mean that they could not have done better, but it was acknowledging that they were human and therefore imperfect. I had to change my perspective before I could change my physical patterns. Understanding this perspective helped me to process my fears of not being wanted and the associated emotions.

Athaliah encouraged me to become vegetarian by showing me how much better I felt when I ate no meat or fish. Within two weeks of committing to a vegetarian diet, the acid reflux had disappeared and I was burping less. When I became comfortable with that, which took about 6 months, she encouraged me to try intermittent fasting, which has evolved to include weekly 24-hour fasts.

My sweet tooth has decreased and I have begun to break the habit of eating sweet food when I am stressed, feeling uncomfortable or unsafe in a new experience. This was the hardest habit to break. I now drink less caffeine, eat less bread (which does not agree with me) and have lots more vegetables and fruit.

She has helped me to find new ways to cook meals and eat delicious food, as well as new ways to exercise. I now have a rebounder which always brings a smile to my face.

She led me to information which helped me understand how to adapt my body and mind. This has inspired me and kept me going on my journey. Mentally, I have more control over my eating habits. I have let go of the beliefs that hindered my weight loss and am comfortable with embracing change and creating new habits to support a healthier body and mind.

This process is still being refined as I write this, so please remember to be patient and kind to your body.

Stubborn weight

Having followed my suggestions, some of you may find that your weight or appearance does not change. You may feel better, look better, and do all the right things, but your tummy has not shrunk, or your thighs do not look as you want them.

You have changed energetically. You are happier, more satisfied and emotionally different, but your physical cells refuse to budge from their fear-based perspective. Remember that this is all energetic. Your cells are not sitting there, with pen and paper, going "Nope, we are not doing that!". They have a habit of being present which needs to be changed. This could be because of fears around identity – who will we be if we lose weight? Or Who will love you, if you let us go? This perspective is based in so much love for you from your cells. And it showing you that there is another layer of healing to be done.

It would be easy to get frustrated with your body and wonder what more you need to do, but that can take you into the energy of punishing your body. This is the time when you need to be more compassionate with yourself. Show more kindness, understanding and love to your physical body. You may want to take up new habits that pamper your body or help you feel alive e.g. ice baths. Listen to your cells they will tell you.

In addition to the gorgeous new habits that make you feel good, you will connect energetically with your physical cells. They are hyper-intelligent and you can talk to them about the changes you want. Ask them to work with you, rather than staying stuck.

You can listen to this audio here

"A conversation with your cells"

The process is given below:

1. Connect with your Higher Self and set the intention to connect with the physical cells in your body. You are going to focus on an area where you would like to see a physical change e.g. your thighs, bottom, arms, tummy, etc.

2. Use your imagination energy to picture yourself sitting somewhere comfortable. It could be a room, a field or a favourite spot you like to visit. You can feel the breeze and the sunshine. It is exactly how you like it.

3. Invite your cells to join you. Explain that you want to understand what prevents them from trusting that they are safe and loved and that it is okay to release the excess weight. Ask them is there anything else that you need to understand in order to let them go. This conversation is not about blame or accusation, it is about listening and understanding what your physical cells need.

4. At this point, you may receive images, one-word answers or phrases. Sit with this, do not rush it. You want to get as much understanding as possible. Repeat this stage if you want to.

5. Ask your physical cells what they need you to do. For example, they may want you to play like a child on the swings or jump off logs because that is when you feel carefree in your body. They may need you to have a bubble bath or make a specific cake or dish which has good memories associated with it. They may need you to go back to the first time you felt abandoned or lost and send love to the past version of you. These actions are important as they emphasise your willingness to work with your body, to listen to its needs and to act accordingly. So please, if you receive an action, be available to act.

6. Finally, ask your Higher Self to help you flow love to your cells from the time you began to gain weight to the present day. This is an unconditional, non-judgemental love. It is the love that connects your body to God. It is the love that

allows you to believe that you are safe, that you will be looked after and that you are here to thrive. It is a powerful, irresistible call to cooperate and return to your healthiest, best-functioning state.

7. Thank your cells and then disconnect.

Repeat this process regularly to help your cells feel supported. Celebrate the changes you notice as you introduce more pampering, fun, movement and acknowledgement of how fabulous your beautiful body is.

I have experienced this stubbornness and, when I worked through this process, I was taken to the emotion of shame, regret and reminded of feeling abandoned. You may not be, but my cells held shame about several experiences, with each event layered onto the next, forming an energetic straitjacket. I have been working through these layers and, by the time I had released the first two, I had dropped 1½ dress sizes!

Cognitive Patterns

Have you ever wanted to do something but your thoughts would not allow it? Or if you did it, your brain seemed to go into a panic?

Whilst visiting a friend in Eire, in November 2023, she casually mentioned going for a swim. I agreed, not realising we were going for a cold-water swim in the Atlantic! It was an experience I wanted to try after watching Chris Hemsworth in his series 'Limitless'.

When I got in the water, my brain went into overdrive. I could feel panic as it constantly said, "We must get out of here, it is not safe."

The reality was that my feet were still on the ground and the water was not even up to my waist. I stayed in the water and even dunked myself. After what felt like a long five minutes, I began to walk back to shore, and I could feel the relief in my thoughts. But more interestingly, I felt that my body did not want to get out of the water. It was happy there, despite the cold. That encouraged me to return to the water and the same thing happened, but not as strongly.

This was a cognitive pattern i.e. a thought that was trying to keep me safe.

You can experience many cognitive patterns. Losing weight may make you feel unsafe because it is unfamiliar, or there may be unpleasant associations of being slimmer when you have felt vulnerable or uncomfortable. Your brain may stop you from trying new things.

It may be easier to imagine a cognitive pattern as an extra layer of clothing wrapped around your body. Do you remember the scene from *'Friends'* when Joey went into Monica's apartment, wearing all of Chandler's clothes? That is a good analogy of multiple cognitive patterns!

Breaking a Cognitive Pattern

Like emotional or mental patterns, cognitive patterns are grounded in the idea of keeping you safe and feeling loved by God. You must energetically release and FORGET the emotions that keep the cognitive pattern going. You may have patterns about your ability to pass exams, study well, achieve promotions or pay rises, as well as others which are health-related or with relationships.

Use this process to clear any cognitive patterns you notice:

You can listen to this audio here.

"Clearing Cognitive Patterns"

1. Connect to your Higher Self.

2. Bring the cognitive pattern to mind and state that you wish to understand what created it. You may see the pattern as a shape or sound wave.

3. You may receive insight via images or words. Allow it to flow fully.

4. Cut the cord that attaches these emotions and memories by using the SIP 'Forget' followed by 'Delete'

5. Notice how the flow of energy feels. If you struggle to remember the pattern, you know it has worked.

6. Thank your Higher Self and let go of the connection.

I have had to release cognitive patterns around shame, regret and grief but, by doing so, I lost weight!

Important Reminder

When you work with your Higher Self on a physical illness or a change you are creating, you must be patient with yourself and your Higher Self. You must be willing to take consistently kind action but also accept there will be times when you must energetically Rest. When you Rest, things are still happening. Rest allows your body to catch up with the Energetics and process what is being asked. This is different to sleep, which is when you enter a dream state and repairs take place.

Energetics and Exercise

Exercise is more than just for losing weight or toning up. It helps the body's systems work better. Historically, when we lived in nomadic tribes, we walked most of the day which kept the body fit and working in good order. Becoming increasingly sedentary has caused problems.

Your physical characteristics are in your soul contract. As we know, your Higher Self is there to help you, so can show you which type of exercise you need to do to create a body you love. You may think you need to run daily, but your Higher Self could show you that Yoga will create the results you are seeking. They can show you the simplest way to achieve the body or fitness levels you want or need. This covers:

- the optimal time for your body to work out

- having fun while exercising so you only generate high vibrations

- knowing what to eat to complement the exercise, before and after your workout

Start by asking yourself the following questions:

- What am I seeking? To accept the body I have in an energy of love or am I seeking a loving change to give me freedom. Freedom for what purpose? To be able to embrace more opportunities to experience life e.g. to become a parent or to bungee jump or to look and feel beautiful in clothes.

- What do I want to look like? Use images to help you identify this.

- Do I want to feel strong and flexible? What kind of physique do I want?

- Do I love exercising?

- What is the best exercise for me to get started?

- When, and how often, should I exercise?

- What should I eat to support my body, through the workouts, so that I am not exhausted?

- What can I do to support my body's recovery?

What is a body that you love?

Each of us has our own definition of health and how we want our body to look. You might be influenced or inspired by images of actors and actresses. That is wonderful but your body is unique and your journey, to a body that you love and cherish, will be different to their journeys. Do not become a slave to trends. Trust your Higher Self's guidance on how to create a body you will love and cherish.

For those of you with health conditions, you might want to reverse these and return to who you were before your illness. I have covered how to reverse illnesses with your Higher Self's help. You can try to return to a version of who you were, but that version no longer exists. Today, it will be a new version who has experienced illness and learned resilience in the face of adversity that you connect with. The needs of this body will be different to the previous one. It may need you to focus on gentle stretching, as it reacquaints itself with movement, before graduating to more challenging exercises.

Your body could be muscular and flexible, or slim and light-footed. Perhaps you are designed to have great aerobic capacity to run and hike as much as you like, for as long as you want. Perhaps you want a curvaceous body to feel sexy and feminine. Your Higher Self can help you with these.

Why is it important to love and cherish this body?

This is important because it avoids punishment energy, as well as condemning thoughts and blame. We mentally rail or question our bodies:

- Why is my body so dry?
- Why is it not doing what I want it to?
- How do I get rid of my belly?
- Why is my body storing fat?

These questions are directed at your body, but you are probably not waiting for the answer. You have to learn to listen better since your physical body has the knowledge it needs, thanks to your soul contract, to be beautiful and shapely.

Your physical body is a beautiful representation of how you are emotionally, mentally and physically. It is the home of your soul. You need to disengage from the idea that you or your body are doing something wrong.

Instead, you want to encourage a two-way conversation with your physical cells. Your Higher Self can help you by:

1. Helping you to cook food that nourishes your cells.

2. Guiding you to the type of exercise that will help your body.

3. Advising about the length of your exercise session.

4. Advising about the frequency of your exercise session.

5. Helping you to evolve your food and exercise regimes, as your body changes in response to the guidance.

6. Releasing limiting beliefs about your body, your ideas around health and your ability to become healthy.

Earlier in this chapter I talked about my carbuncle. The final part of my healing was when I acknowledged how amazing my body was. Not only had it been holding those strong emotions of anger, rage, sadness, grief, and judgement, but it had managed to put them into one place, the cyst, to protect the rest of my body. Within days of the cause of these emotions being dealt with, I was helped to physically remove the festering feelings via the carbuncle from my body.

I talked to my cells daily, thanking them for all they did and telling them how amazing they were. That it was safe for them to release those feelings I no longer needed. I told them that I loved them and flooded them with my love.

The process of creating a body you love

Appreciation: Take a look at how your body has been evolving and changing since you were in the womb. Acknowledge that many processes happen without you even noticing i.e. breathing, digestion, blood and lymph flow, and how your body maintains the correct pH and temperature while fighting off infections. It is utterly amazing!

Gratitude: Start by thanking your body every morning and every evening for all it has done. Each part works in perfect order from getting ready in the morning, to the way your fingers tap the keys on your keyboard, to how your senses show you the beauty of the world, and so much more. Admire your limbs, your tummy and your chest as they are now. Do not wait for them to be what you deem as perfect. If you feel able to, admire your body in the mirror. Become familiar with your lumps and bumps, as they are signposts of your journey so far.

Talk to your body: It may take a while to understand its response but persist. One way to do this is by asking your Higher Self, "What is the simplest thing I can do to help you today?" Then listen. Notice any urges e.g. drink more water, eat an apple or even some chocolate. The more you practise this, the easier communication will become. Your cells can be helped to understand your goal if you think of a visual e.g. an athlete, actor or someone you know personally.

Exercise: Write a love letter to your body with your Higher Self's help. This could be a simple note that says, "I'm sorry that I ate the wrong food yesterday" or "I love you". It could be a longer letter in which you explore your feelings about your tummy, abdominal muscles or biceps, and what it means to you to have a strong beautiful body.

You may want to write to yourself, from the future, congratulating yourself on achieving that strong, healthy or flexible body and how confident you feel. Ideally, write a note or a letter every day to build the momentum you need to act and create the changes you want. It may feel hard to do that initially but, I promise, it will quickly become a habit if you allow it.

Store the letters and use them for inspiration when you struggle to keep to your plan.

Choose to follow through: Act on your understanding. Action is always required but the one you are being asked to do may not be what you expect. For example, if you have a lot of weight to lose, you may think your body wants to try a high-intensity training session. But when you communicate with your body, you understand it may want you to drink more water and do belly dancing! If you want to gain weight or look stronger, your physical cells may want you to improve your protein sources so that you are better able to absorb them.

My background in holistic health makes me encourage you to look at the whole picture i.e. the emotional, mental, and physical picture. I will always encourage you to take control of your health. You now have the knowledge and understanding of how to feel better energetically. You know how to release stored emotions and break cycles of thought. You also know that you must take physical action to rewrite your neural patterns.

Love your body fiercely

Your body deserves the changes you can help it make. It is a fabulous home for your soul and has been helping you cope with life magically, without you even realising it. It is time to love it back and let it thrive.

My final gift to you is an energetic process called *Love your Body*. It will help you to feel better about it as it is right now and, combined with the other processes, it can help you make great changes.

Listen to this practice here.

"Love your Body"

Energetics and Grief

Grief comes in many forms e.g. the death of someone we love, the life we wished we could have lived, our experiences, as well as a multitude of emotions, such as:

Sorrow	Anger	Hate
Pity	Loss of Hope	Loneliness

It feels like a heavy weight that literally weighs you down. It is insidious as it seeps into everything you experience daily and reminds you of what you have lost. Grief can rob you of the desire to live life because it just feels too hard. It can stop you from connecting to feeling enthusiastic about life and joy in the moment.

If you have had a difficult journey through life, there will be a layer of grief that needs to be released. Your journey may include horrible childhood experiences or the death of a pet or person who was important to you.

This grief can permeate every physical cell in your body, as well as your energetic framework. If you have worked with your Higher Self, you will have released some grief but, by clearing this layer, you will find it easier to experience joy and feel that life is for living.

When you are ready, your Higher Self will take you to the place to release this grief. They will show you when it is time. My experience of that was when Athaliah kept showing me things that reminded me of my dad, who died in 2011, as well as painful experiences in my childhood.

Since I am human, my first reaction was to feel anger and confusion. I thought, "What the F...? I do not want to experience this again!"

But, with huge love and compassion, Athaliah persisted and showed me that, in letting go of my grief, I could step out of the shadows and allow myself to be who I truly am. In a way, it has led to this book being written and published!

Grief will change you forever and you will grow from the experience, but you have a choice to make:

- How will you react to this?

- Will you allow yourself to drown in the grief or will you allow yourself to grow?

Following my dad's death, I was drowning in my grief for almost six months but, eventually, with the help of a bereavement counsellor, I made the choice to live. That choice led to many changes and experiences I would not give up for the world.

I am not going to give you a step-by-step process to help you heal from your grief, because that is a journey to undertake with your Higher Self. By now, your relationship should be solid, and you should be able to trust the guidance given. Remember to be patient and kind to yourself and if necessary, ask for help

Take a deep breath and dive straight in. The rewards will be worth it and you will then understand the adage:

Life is for Living (rather than just existing)

Energetics and a Terminal Diagnosis

If you are diagnosed with a terminal illness, you can use Energetics to make peace with your diagnosis and find a way to maximise the time you have left on Earth.

Receiving a terminal diagnosis can be devastating for you and your family and friends. But, if you can find acceptance and ease in the diagnosis, you will be more content in your final months.

I believe that, by doing so, you will allow yourself to experience life in a vastly different way. Instead of being filled with grief, you can choose with the help of your Energetics to fill your final months with laughter, love and beautiful conversations which culminate in a high vibrational transition.

I am not ignoring or minimising the diagnosis or the impact, but you can control how you respond to it. You can choose to go to pieces and feel devastated until you die, or you can go to pieces and then say, "Enough, I want to make the most of the time that is left."

Neither is wrong, but both are a choice. When you stay in a state of devastation, resisting what is happening, your energy is expended to maintain the resistance and fear.

It will be hard to do but focus on keeping your vibrations high. If you have been talking to your Higher Self, releasing your limiting beliefs, as well as noticing and changing your thoughts, you will have the tools to bring balance and calm. You will be surprised how quickly those tools will help.

Sometimes, when you maintain a high vibration, you will exceed the expectations of the medical community and receive more time than anticipated. New opportunities for treatments or alternative solutions may become available because of your high vibration. Maintaining this will bring a sense of control, peace and acceptance.

How can your Higher Self help you come to terms with your Diagnosis?

Your soul contract was created before you were born as a physical human and contains details of how you will transition. This is not set in stone because you have free will to live your life as you wish and ignore your contract through the choices you make.

Some choices will create low-stored vibration which brings disease to the body. When you get the diagnosis, you may feel devastated and wish you had made better choices.

Your Higher Self can help you release regrets and make peace with where you are now, which may mean your physical life is ending. That is okay because we are here for a limited time. When we transition back to a non-physical state, we will share this physical life with the rest of our non-physical family – our Higher Self, our families who have already transitioned and the Higher Self collectives.

Energetics and Death

You can choose the nature of your death. Will it be a peaceful, joyful passing or a traumatic one where you resist what is coming? I am not saying that if you get a terminal diagnosis, you should just give up and die. You can choose how you want to pass.

In this situation, you can choose to make peace with where you are now or stay fearful and scared. It is not easy but it is simple.

A good death is a beautiful gift you can give yourself, your friends and family. By allowing yourself to find peace and ease with the finality of your physical life, you reduce the fear that your friends and family may have around death and your transition from this physical plane. Of course, they will still miss you and mourn but they will remember the time with you as a golden experience, filled with love and hope.

If you have been developing your relationship with your Higher Self, your transition will bring a beautiful reunion with them and your family who have gone before. While this may not be something you focus on, let it be a comforting thought in the background.

The Love Connection

One of the things we fear as humans is losing the love of the person who transitions. We fear being alone, being lonely, and being lost. But here is the magic, you can remain connected through love. When you go to your sacred space with your Higher Self and centre yourself, they can help you connect with your loved ones. It can be upsetting. It took me almost ten years to hold the connection to my dad. Before that, I would get so distressed that I could not continue.

1. Close your eyes and connect to Your Higher Self.

2. Ask them to take you to your sacred space, which will be different for each of you. For some, it will be in the depths of the ocean and, for others, it will be in a forest or mountains.

3. At the entrance of your sacred space is your Watcher who will look after you whilst you enter.

4. Greet them and let them know your intention.

5. They will open the door and allow you to pass into the sacred space.

6. Find a comfortable spot and invite your relative or friend in.

7. When you have finished your conversation, bid your loved one farewell and head back to your gate.

8. Step out and say goodbye to your Watcher.

9. Walk back to your reality with your Higher Self.

10. Open your eyes and take a drink of water. Water helps to ground you back into physical reality.

You can repeat this process as often as you wish.

Summary

Your health reflects your life's experiences which have generated low stored or low transitional vibrations. Left untreated, these can result in ill health.

You can connect with your Higher Self to release these low vibrations and the impact of those experiences to contribute to your healing.

Energetics work well with conventional medicine and can improve your response to medication, as well as your recovery.

Find a place of ease with any diagnosis to start your recovery from a love-based perspective.

Bless the people who work with you on your recovery and any medication.

Once you have cleared the energetic limitations, you may need to improve communication with your physical body to create change.

Notice any cognitive patterns.

Your Higher Self can guide you on how to eat well, exercise in a way your body will respond to and improve your overall health.

Love your body fiercely.

You can choose how you react to a terminal diagnosis and what your death experience will be like.

Your loved ones who have passed are still connected to you through their love for you.

8

ENERGETICS EVERY DAY AND FAMILY

The definition of family, in this instance, includes your biological family, foster or adoptive families, friends, pets, community and culture you are born into and the planet.

In your soul contract, you made agreements with other souls about the role they would play in your life. Some souls will agree to be lifelong friends, others for a few days or weeks. Some souls will enter your life to teach life lessons, to help you grow or evolve, or for you to teach them. Others will be your greatest supporters. Pets are known as spiritual companions. They are here to support you and show you how to live in the moment, in the most loving way possible.

What do you want to achieve with Energetics and Family?

Self-acceptance is the aim since this is the basis of the principle, 'Love for ME first'.

Our judgements about ourselves are often based on external values placed on us. Our immediate families and cultures will have opinions about gender, education, what is considered appropriate or not, and they will be clear about what they consider acceptable in us. The media, especially social media, also has an influence. When we base our judgement on these external factors, we forget our worthiness and that we are here with purpose and not by accident.

Our families are not inherently bad people, including those who are abusive. Before you throw the book against the wall, please hear me out. We are all products of our environment. We may have been abandoned, ignored or ridiculed. We have probably all experienced loss or rejection, as well as a desire to be acknowledged and loved. It is from a perspective of feeling insignificant and unworthy that people often act inappropriately or in a way that is just wrong. They become overwhelmed by the hurt and lash out. This does not justify their abusive behaviours or make them acceptable, but it may give an insight into why they behave as they do.

For most people, a lack of loving self-acceptance shows up as poor boundaries; being prepared to accept less in relationships or it may show us as additive or controlling behaviour. It may show up as addictive behaviour or control.

Communication is one of our biggest challenges when dealing with family. The words we say can be uplifting or devastating. We can hurt each other with our words or our silence. Those words can feed our fears of being unloved for who we are, or not being wanted or seen. Those words can make us feel unfavourably compared to our siblings or peers, and we want to hide.

Remember that everyone's vibration is made up of their experiences, whether biological, fostered, adoptive or cultural, as well as their genetic memory. These contribute to your personal and familial vibrations. Everyone will have unique low, transitional and high vibrations stored in their bodies and minds, and as you interact physically so do your vibrations.

In one course, I was stunned when I connected to a genetic cultural memory, to release it. I was being led through a visualisation when I heard hundreds of voices wailing in my head. When I asked what it was, it was a genetic memory of the West Bengal Famine of 1943, which killed around three million people. My family is from West Bengal and my mum and dad were born during that time.

Imagine the effect on families of watching children, the elderly and others dying from a lack of food. That famine was not a natural disaster but a direct result of orders from Winston Churchill.

For Bengalis, food is a subject we love to talk about, often discussing our next meal as we eat the current one. The guilt felt by survivors and the constant worry about food availability created a huge impact on the cellular and genetic memory of the West Bengal population.

When you work with your Higher Self to find self-acceptance, the Releasing Process helps you deal with any anger and hurt that surfaces. It also helps you experience compassion for your journey, as well as for those who have affected it. You begin to understand that they have been operating the only way they could, with the information they had at the time, and which is often based on fear.

Circles of Love

You are the start of the Circle of Love because everything flows from you. Therefore, when using Energetics, there should always be a benefit to you. It should feel loving, as well as help you to receive more love. **Energetics is for YOU FIRST**, so do not use it solely for the benefit of others as this will make what you create small. You are as worthy and deserving of all you desire as the next person. If you perpetuate the myth that others are more important, more worthy or more capable than you, it will unbalance your energy and may cause a physical reaction. Embrace your worthiness and the perfection of who you are, as a physical human, although it does not mean you will not get things wrong. Embrace your worthiness and the perfection of who you are, as a physical human, although it does not mean you will not get things wrong.

Everyday Energetics and Family

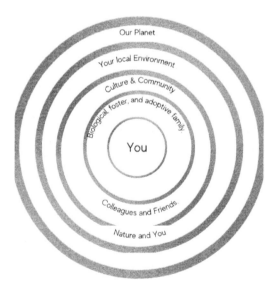

It All Starts with You.

Unconditional Love

Unconditional love is the love of the Divine which does not judge or criticise. It acknowledges that every person is deserving of love, no matter what they have said or done to you. They are a soul, having a human experience, and due to a perspective of fear and disconnection, they have made mistakes.

This chapter will deal with sending unconditional love. If this feels challenging, start by sending it to yourself.

Place your hands over your heart, connect to your Higher Self and ask to receive a flow of unconditional love. You may fall asleep as you relax deeply, or you may become emotional or feel wired. Go with whatever comes, as it will be the perfect reaction for you.

How can Energetics Help with Family?

1. Energetics can give an understanding

By connecting to the energy flow, you can receive a sense of what the other person is feeling or experiencing, which can influence how you feel. You may have more compassion for them, the situation and yourself. You may be able to forgive them or yourself. This is immensely powerful in helping you move through difficult situations.

For example, a person appears to be emotionally down. When you connect with your Higher Self, you may be shown that they are seething with anger, feeling isolated or unwanted. This can affect how you feel about them and allow you to feel compassion.

Exercise:

- Sit comfortably in a quiet place.

- Connect to your Higher Self and ask to be connected with a specific family member and their Higher Self.

- Ask to be shown how they are feeling. You may receive an image or words like vulnerable, scared, confident, or strong.

- Repeat this with each member of your family.

- When you have finished, open your eyes and have a drink of water.

2. Energetics can help with communication

Scientists estimate that 85% of our communication is non-verbal. With the help of our Higher Self, we can communicate with our family energetically about how we are feeling and the outcome we hope for.

Exercise:

- Connect to your Higher Self, ask to be connected to the person you wish to talk to energetically, and their Higher Self. You can do this in your Sacred Space if you wish.

- Once you see them (in your mind's eye), tell them honestly how you are feeling and how you would like the relationship to be.

- Imagine that they are responding. What are they saying? What feeling is emanating from them?

You can be candid and truthful in this conversation. Their Higher Self will translate it to them on an unconscious level. They will feel the truth of your words and a nudge to change. A lovely truth for someone in this energetic space is: "The Truth is that I accept you as you are."

This truth may be challenging to you. When you accept the person as they are, you are not asking them to change to make you feel better. This is a powerful and loving perspective to share with others.

Will it make a difference?

It can, although it may take a while to notice any changes. The other person has free will to ignore their Higher Self or any nudges they may feel to compromise, soften or apologise. But it will make you feel better – and that is an excellent place to be.

3. Energetics can improve relationships

Energetic communication can create subtle changes in relationships because you are flowing in the truest version of yourself; the most loving, unconditional, and accepting version. Thus, you can see others the same way.

One of the loveliest things you can do is to flow unconditional love to your family, especially those who have angered you. It will flow from you to your Higher Self, to their Higher Self and then to that person.

If you have been practising the work suggested in this book, you will no longer be in the same place energetically. You will be operating from a perspective of love. This is unconditional and will help your family feel better. When they feel better, they behave better, feeling safe and acknowledged. This can create beautiful high vibrations and change negative experiences to positive ones.

You can flow unconditional love to anyone. When I practised Reiki, I would send this love to random celebrities, three times. The beauty of this was that I knew nothing about them or what was happening behind the image, so I had to trust that the flow of Reiki (unconditional love) was going where it needed to.

For those of you who are not familiar with Reiki, let me give a brief explanation. Think of the various energy based modalities as operating on different frequencies. To practise Reiki, you must be attuned to its specific frequency by a Reiki Master Teacher. Attunements are not required to work with your Higher Self, making Energetics accessible to all.

One such celebrity was Britney Spears. The flow was really strong and I wondered why, when it looked like she was riding high. I sent it to her over three weeks. Eventually, I stopped, as life took over. It was soon afterwards that her public meltdown began. It made me realise that everyone can benefit from unconditional love. I now do this with the flow of Energetics and my Higher Self Athaliah, rather than Reiki.

On a recent journey, I noticed that the man opposite me looked tense and stressed. I connected with Athaliah and started to flow unconditional love to him. About ten minutes later, I noticed that he began smiling and laughing to himself. I had helped to shift some low transitional vibrations in him. You will be able to do this with practice.

I like to know that the people around me are feeling good and I make the time to focus on sending them unconditional love.

4. Energetics can improve boundaries and self-love

When you practise the flow of Energetics and release your limiting beliefs, your vibration rises. You are choosing to love yourself more and first.

You begin to notice more acutely what, or who, makes you feel better or happier, and you will choose to hang out with them more. Or you might decide that spending time alone is the most loving thing to do. You can find yourself with more boundaries around how you spend your time. You may notice that you are more compassionate and loving towards yourself. This is the principle of 'Love for You First', which is similar to the idea of putting your oxygen mask on before trying to help others.

As you start showing this energy of loving yourself and putting yourself first, you will challenge and discombobulate others and they may react. For example, you may decide to stop drinking alcohol. People may find this challenging and pick an argument or stop inviting you to social events. They do not understand that you are not doing this to provoke them but to love yourself more. Their reaction is based on their low vibration and perspective that they may need alcohol to have a good time.

When I became a vegetarian, it challenged some in my close family circle as they felt they could not feed me well (food is a love language in my culture). I focused on healing my body and it was the perfect way for me to do it.

Discombobulation may happen because you are energetically calling them to join you. Some will pick an argument or stop talking to you, but others will gladly join you. You may notice that you see less of some friends, but more of others. Members of your biological family may no longer want to talk to you, or vice versa. That allows you to flow with the following principles which put you first and help you feel loved and loving towards yourself.

Love for You First

Do not go where Love does not flow

These help you to live a connected high-vibrational life, filled with happiness, flow and ease.

5. Energetics can help improve the energy levels of others

You can use your Energetics to help family members by introducing the idea that, if the energy changes, so does the outcome to them. Only do this with people who you think will be receptive.

Remember, family encompasses more than just your biological family.

In 2022, my mother-in-law was living with us and was very unwell. I took her to the local A&E department and, after the initial triage, we were told to wait for about three hours. While waiting to be seen, I wondered what I could do to help energetically, and was nudged to flow unconditional love to all the NHS staff working that day.

I closed my eyes and asked Athaliah to help me connect to the Higher Selves of everyone at work in the A&E department, including X-ray and reception, the nurses, doctors and orderlies. I then flowed unconditional love to them, with the intention that it would help them do their jobs well. I could have used the flow of Energetics to get my mother-in-law seen more quickly, but it did not occur to me!

I flowed this energy for approximately 5-10 minutes and then let it go. I then flowed the same to everyone sitting in A&E with us, for about five minutes, so they would feel at ease in waiting.

We were called within thirty minutes, instead of the expected three hours, and everyone was super helpful. The top oncologist was called in to see my mother-in-law and she was admitted by a lovely doctor.

When I spoke to my mentor at the time, she commented that, by flowing unconditional love to everyone, I had helped improve their energy levels and, therefore, their efficiency. The energy had helped them to feel appreciated which translated into better care for patients in the A&E department.

Another example involves my husband, who travels daily on the motorway to work. Often this journey ends up being over two hours each way because of accidents. When I asked if the accidents happened at a specific place, he mentioned a junction called Maple Cross. When I tuned into the energy of the place, it looked like a car junkyard. Each time there was an accident, it added to the energy of the car junkyard which, in turn, acted like an energetic beacon, causing more accidents. It was essentially becoming a self-fulfilling cycle. I could feel how the resources of the emergency services and local hospitals were stretched by these accidents.

Using the SIP 'Dissipate' on this energy, I asked that it be replaced with an easy and steady flow and that the emergency services and hospitals benefit too. Within five days, my husband's journey had improved and the number of reported accidents were reduced.

6. Energetics can help romantic relationships

Many of us have been raised with the idea of the 'other half' in our romantic relationships. I do not subscribe to that model. I prefer being the best version of myself and my husband being the best version of himself. We then bring these into our relationship. This means that you both have to work on your personal development, which can be in many forms. I recommend that you ask your Higher Self for the simplest way to do this.

My husband has chosen a different way to develop which best suits his energy. That is his free will and there is an enormous sense of freedom when you feel comfortable enough to let your special person find their way. You are not responsible for their growth.

You are responsible for:

- Showing up as the best version of you; not necessarily the happiest, but the most authentic version.

- Having clear and kind communication with your partner.

- Committing daily to your relationship. You can do this in many ways, by cooking their favourite dish, doing the laundry or sending a loving message. It could be asking for space i.e. a day or a week where you do what is important to you. In that space, you will realise again that your partner is your special person. If you are in a committed relationship, I am not advocating that you date other people!

Be honest about limiting beliefs and notice how they play out in your relationship. If you were raised in a home where love and attention were inconsistent, do you now struggle to accept consistent love and attention? Or if you grew up in a home where shouting then silence was the norm, do you instigate fights and then withdraw in an angry silence? This is deep work but, by committing to it and breaking down potential barriers, you will protect your relationship from sabotage. The Releasing Process and your Higher Self can help clear these beliefs and behaviours.

7. Energetics can connect you to transitioned loved ones

Ask your Higher Self to connect and take you to your sacred space which is your personal energetic space. My space is like a garden with an orchard, amazing views and a bench. Yours could be underwater, in a city in the sky or on a beach. It will be different for each of you.

Your Watcher guards the entrance to your sacred space so that you will not be disturbed. Greet them as you approach, then step inside. Ask your Higher Self to come and invite your family member to join you.

This experience can feel very comforting. I have used it to connect with my dad and various other members of my family. Friends have also connected with their loved ones.

You can listen to this audio here.

"Connecting to your Sacred Space"

8. Energetics can help you enter the Chamber of God

The Chamber of God is another energy space which will appear different to each of you. For some, it is a beautiful place filled with colour and movement. For me, I feel nothing more about the space other than knowing it is safe.

Your Higher Self can help you enter the chamber of God and create a circle of love. This is used to communicate with a group of people in the circle and flow unconditional love to each of them.

The circle is about showing up as you truly are. Not encumbered with grief, hate or anger, but the person you are at a soul level, who is joyful, loving, kind, compassionate, etc. Sometimes you will want to go into the circle to help them understand the changes in you. At other times, it will be to flow love to them, just because you can, and you want them to feel better. Or it could be to call them to feel better and change habits. This is all done with an energy of love.

Who do you call to the circle of love?

- Members of your biological/adoptive family
- Colleagues

- Teammates

- Customers

- Friends

- Spiritual companions i.e. your pets

- Anyone you will interact with in your day

You can call colleagues and teammates to be their best selves, so that collaborating with them is more enjoyable, effective and fun, with great outcomes. By flowing love to them, you will help them to feel safe and valued.

This can be a fun exercise as you send them love once a week and see how they respond. You might notice a more relaxed atmosphere or more laughter, with more work being done. A member of staff, who is difficult to work with due to their low vibration energy, may go off sick. You may question how that is a loving action, but they probably need time to rest and recover. By continuing to send them love, they may have a physical reaction and their vibration will rise sufficiently for them to return. Notice is there a change in them – are they happier or more sociable or more relaxed - and update your evidence log.

With customers, you already have a soul contract to deliver a product or service. In the circle of love, you can let them know that you are ready to fulfil the contract and are calling them lovingly to work with you. Some of you may feel inspired to use relevant SIPs (Spiritual Intention Protocols) to help your customers.

You could try it with people you do not know e.g. politicians or celebrities but remember that you will not necessarily feel or notice a change in their behaviour or outcomes. When you flow unconditional love to strangers you interact with in shops or by phone, you will help them to feel good and, in turn, you will get a better service.

For each person in the circle of love, you should also invite their Higher Selves. Then the love will flow from you to your Higher Self, on to their Higher Self and, finally, to them.

You can listen to this audio here.

"Connecting to a Circle of Love"

9. Energetics can break generational patterns of behaviour

I learned about this when I studied Level 2 of Usui Reiki. In those days, I would connect to Reiki but now I ask Athaliah to help, as it feels more direct and more effective.

Many families have generational behaviour patterns around food, alcohol, abuse, money, etc. You can break these addictive patterns as they no longer serve you or your family.

If there is more than one person involved, you can break the pattern in a circle of love but always start with yourself.

Exercise: Connect to your Higher Self and ask to be shown the pattern that exists within you around your addiction or experience. Then ask for unconditional love to be sent to the first person in your family line in whom this pattern emerged. It may be a woman or a man and might have happened several generations ago. You may get a sense of what they felt then;

maybe trapped, scared or powerless. You may receive an image of them wrapped in a chain or another description of their experience.

Ask your Higher Self to help you flow unconditional love to them and imagine it as a stream of golden light moving through the generations to that person. Surrounded by the golden light, see them energetically healed and released from the pattern. As they are, so are the subsequent generations. You may get a beautiful vision of chains falling away or your ancestors smiling as they are freed from this burden of behaviour and you will feel lighter and freer.

Once you have energetically released your ancestors and yourself, check with your physical cells that they have also released the pattern, as detailed in Chapter 7 Energetics Every Day and Your Health.

If there are other people in your family with the same ancestral line, you can ask for the healing to be shared with them. It will involve slightly more work if they are not.

Connect to your Higher Self and ask to be connected to that person's Higher Self. Ask permission to break the cycle (if the person has not verbally asked you to do this). If you do not receive a clear 'yes' or 'no' do not continue as the free will of the other person is important.

If you get a 'yes', repeat the process of connecting with their ancestor who developed the pattern and then flow healing as written above.

Remember to manage the other person's expectations as this is not a miracle cure but a step on their journey to health and prosperity.

Example: If your family has ever been enslaved, there will be an unconscious connection that could appear in your daily life via communication, achievements or behaviour. You may feel that you can never quite control your destiny or feel free. You can ask your Higher Self to release those chains of slavery from the first ancestor who was enslaved. You may be shown an image of a plantation or a slave ship. You may see that person in chains. Ask your Higher Self to flow love and freedom to your ancestor. Imagine the chains falling off as they stand up straight and stretch. See them looking strong and empowered once more, free to choose their destiny.

As you do this, you may see more chains falling off other ancestors and a sense of freedom will grow within you. As each of your ancestors is released from their chains, understand that you too are being released and empowered to live your life authentically. This will show up as changes in your behaviour, confidence and interactions.

10.   Energetics can affect world events

We are part of humanity as a whole, so the term 'family' also applies here. As I author this book, I am conscious that the world is in a struggle between the old and the new.

Brexit was a desire by some to turn back the clock to a golden time in the UK's history to *'Make Britain Great Again'.* The rise of religious conservatism, combined with right-wing politics, has led to the erosion of women's rights across the world, most noticeably in the USA with reproductive rights denied to many. Young people no longer want to subscribe to the old 20th-century model of how we lived. They want freedom and choice, as well as meaning and purpose. They are trying to pull us forward but older generations are pulling backwards, leading to the tussle we see on the bigger world stage.

From an energetic standpoint, it feels like something new is trying to come forward and the old is resisting the potential change. We have all experienced change and know that it can feel scary.

By using Energetics, you can help soothe this fear of change and bring it about in the easiest way. You will not know the minutiae, but you will know that if you approach this from a perspective of love, that embodies compassion for all and hope for better, you cannot go wrong. Change does not have to be hard; we can help birth a new world with ease and love.

Let us take some real-world examples to illustrate this point. When you have read these accounts, you may send Energetics to the examples, which would be brilliant. The more unconditional love we can send the better, so that the change can be more quickly effected.

There have been conflicts in the Middle East, Russia and Ukraine for thousands of years, going back to when they lived in nomadic tribes, and even earlier. When I wrote about my husband's journey to work, I mentioned how the energy had increased in the geographical area. It is the same in these conflicts. From the first skirmish (possibly between just two people) to the tribal battles, to today when we have countries at war, the energy will have built up. Layer upon layer, until it becomes a constantly burning ember, needing only a spark to combust.

By sending Energetics, we aim to achieve balance, peace, reconnection, communication, understanding, compassion and a restoration of hope.

Exercise: Connect to your Higher Self and ask for help to clear this build-up of energy by directing it back to the first event. We do not need to know what it was, only to acknowledge that it happened. Notice what you see, feel or just know. Some of you will get a sense of time of how far the conflict goes back, others will get an image of warring factions or something more abstract. Some will connect with the pain and suffering and the underlying hope and desire for peace. You may notice that the Earth wants to be involved in this healing. This is part of your evidence, so please make a note of it.

Ask for unconditional love to be directed to this first event to heal it. Once healed (the energy will know when), ask for the healing of all subsequent skirmishes, battles or wars. You must remain compassionate and aligned with the idea of unconditional love.

After a few minutes, notice how the conflict feels. Does it feel constricted or conflicted? Does it feel like a change has happened? When I have sent energy to conflicts, I have felt the energy become brighter and lighter. Again, keep a note. If you do not feel anything, do not worry. Just assume that it is having an impact.

By directing unconditional love to this area, we seek peace, kindness, originality of thought for a better solution for those who can implement it and compassion for their fellow men. You do not need to know how that will show up and you are not trying to orchestrate anything or take sides. Your work is to send unconditional love, which is powerful.

You will never know the effects of this love. There will be ripples of peace flowing out to other countries, attempts at ground level to bridge the divides, and people consciously choosing to lay down their arms. Millions of tiny actions will occur because you sent love energetically to bring balance and peace to those areas.

If the energy is changed, the physical experience must change. By living with the fear of pain, being hurt or losing power, our very essence can be lost, which is our humanity. This is not about religion or who is right or wrong, and you are not taking sides. In fact, you are trying to rise above the human pain, guilt, sadness and lack of hope, to help restore kindness, compassion and humanity. You can apply this process to any conflict in the world.

There may be no clear evidence of a sudden massive change but look for the glimmers. It might be an article about mothers from both sides rising to unite or a lessening of restrictions to allow the supply of food and water. These will be your evidence of change.

Check the energy regularly to witness any changes and see if it needs any SIPs. Remember that things are happening behind the scenes, and trust that everything will work out perfectly.

11.   Energetics can affect the environment

Humans are responsible for looking after this beautiful planet but are the biggest polluters. This is our home and part of our family. There are lots of ways you can help it.

On a small scale: if you have any outdoor space, plant insect-friendly plants for the pollinators. Before you plant the seeds or seedlings, place them between your hands and connect to your Higher Self, allowing love to flow to the- it's like an energetic grow more. Flow them with your appreciation of their beauty, scent, place in nature and for what they will add to your environment. This will help them to flourish.

If you like an experiment, divide your seeds and seedlings into two piles. Connect to your Higher Self and ask to flow unconditional love to one pile and nothing to the other. Plant and water them in the same way and see what happens. Photographic evidence would be brilliant for you to see if there is a difference.

You may be passionate about a specific area of nature, such as rivers, and want to help clean them. Ask your Higher Self how to accomplish this locally and allow them to flow nudges and ideas to you. They may encourage you to speak to a local group or attend a workshop. Make sure you act on the nudges because energy + action = change.

On a medium scale: You may feel passionate about local green spaces or want your local council to do more. Again, connect with your beautiful Higher Self and ask to be shown how you can help improve your local environment. Suggestions may be:

- To flow energy to the councillors to help make the environment a priority.

- An idea that inspires you to act e.g. getting together with your neighbours to adopt solar panels, consider water conservation or plant local wildflowers on verges.

- Inspiration to join community activities to meet like-minded people and get involved long-term.

Your Higher Self has access to the right information you need.

On a large scale: You may be devastated by the deforestation of the Amazon or by the fate of the orangutan. By connecting to your Higher Self, ask to be connected to the Earth's energy. This is a beautiful and vast energy with its own wisdom. Ask how you can help bring balance to the Amazon rainforest and listen for the response. You may be surprised about what you are asked to do. Do not assume it will be to flow energy, as that might only be one step. You may be guided by the Earth and your Higher Self to:

- learn more about the subject.

- contact logging companies to understand their viewpoint or what they do to replenish the forests.

- research which companies or charities are working to rebalance the environment.

Have you noticed that when you flow Energetics to the world, conflicts or environment, you seek balance, peace, compassion and connection? Working with the environment rather than against it. This is how we should see each other, as human beings, not as the enemy. When we embrace our humanity, it is the most loving thing we can do for ourselves and creates a massive Circle of Love.

This is our precious planet and it deserves our love and care. As we continue to experience it more and learn to live in a perspective of love, we realise that the Earth is part of our family and also deserves our unconditional love.

A final word

Do not be impatient. Sometimes when we flow energy, there is no apparent immediate effect. Do not be disheartened. Instead, acknowledge that you have flowed energy in the most beautiful way to create balance.

Trust that the universe knows what it is doing and everything will work out perfectly.

Summary

The definition of family is wider than you think.

Your objective is to experience 'Love for Me First' and self-acceptance.

Create circles of love in all you do.

Sending unconditional love is a powerful way to create change and bring comfort.

You can influence your environment positively through Energetics and your Higher Self. They can aid understanding and communication, release generational trauma, and help others to feel better.

Love your planet.

9

ENERGETICS EVERY DAY AND YOUR MONEY

What is your money story and how do you feel about it?

Do you love, dislike, or even hate it?

Do you worry that it will not turn up or will not last?

How do you spend yours and is it enough to help you prosper?

The issue of money can be a minefield and is often related to feelings of self-worth. Many people experience shame around the subject of money. They feel ignorant because they don't know how to improve their money circumstances. Some feel embarrassed by their wealth status compared to others.

It is also related to what you feel you deserve and how much you allow yourself to receive, not just in currency but also in love.

- Do you allow yourself to have help or push it away?
- Do you feel that you do not deserve your place, or will not be valued unless you do everything for everyone?

Your story will also include:

- Your experience with money
- Your family history regarding money
- Observing how others spend their money
- Observing how they talk about money

Culturally, if you grew up in the 1980s and 1990s, the motto *'Greed is Good'* was heavily promoted in the UK & USA. This led to the rampant materialism we see today. To be clear, I am not suggesting that materialism is good or bad. You have free choice of how you spend your money. 😊

All these things contribute to your story. Your own experience with money is the most important.

"Money does not grow on trees" and "Be careful how you spend money because we do not have enough" are refrains many of us have grown up with. But the reality was that the people who said these statements had a poverty mindset.

Money is also linked to how you feel about yourself. Do you feel rich or poor? Do you believe "beggars can't be choosers?" or do you believe "the world is my oyster?" Has experience led you to believe that life is easier for others? If you do not clear up your feelings around money, you can have a huge income yet still feel poor and discontent.

You are here to thrive and prosper. But life experience and limiting beliefs can lead to a strong perspective of fear about your ability to generate currency (cash available to spend). It can lead to periods of contraction i.e. not enough money coming in and, at other times, a deluge of currency. How you manage these periods will create a layer on top of the other experiences and beliefs you have that shape your money story.

Money can leave you feeling frustrated, angry or desperate, which I understand. Although, this does not change your money story or how much currency you can bring into your experience.

The following exercise should help you understand where you are in your money story.

Exercise: Every month or quarter, set aside 30 minutes to answer these questions:

- What is my money story?

- What needs to change for me to create more ease and allow the flow around money and currency?

Without editing, write down your thoughts and allow them to flow as an unfiltered stream of consciousness. If nothing flows at first, keep writing the question above repeatedly. Eventually, you will start to write your answer. This can be powerful, and your Higher Self can nudge you in the right direction. ☺

- Feel the flow of Money Energy to you – is it fast-flowing or sluggish?

- Feel the energy of your bank account – is it tired? Does it need a change? Use SIPs to clear up any tired stagnant energy.

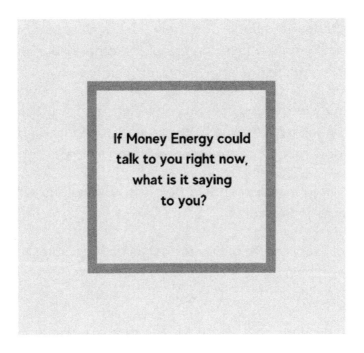

If Money Energy could
talk to you right now,
what is it saying
to you?

Depending upon what you have written, ask these follow-up questions:

- Is there a product or service that will help me understand how money flows through my accounts?
- How can I allow money energy to flow to me more easily?
- What is the simplest action I can take to improve the flow?

Mindset

Your money story will indicate if you have a poverty mindset or an abundant mindset. Your mindset reflects your thoughts and beliefs, not your bank account balance. Do you agree with any of the following statements? Put a mark next to each one and count the total.

Poverty Mindset	Abundant Mindset	
Always feels poor	Always knows there is more coming	
Never feels they are getting ahead	Understands that growth is incremental	
Feels they have to work really hard	Knows there are lots of ways to receive	
Struggles to trust all will work out	Completely trusts that everything will work out	
Surplus money is spent now	Plans for the future	
Cannot see any opportunities	Sees lots of opportunities	

If you have more ticks in the first column, there is work to do. Depending on your desires, you may still have work to do even if you had more marks in the abundant mindset column.

Below is a list of limiting beliefs in a poverty mindset:

- There is never enough money to go around

- Money does not last

- Money is the root of all evil

- I do not deserve to be compensated for my services

- Health and wealth do not go together

- The rich only get richer and the poor get poorer
- It is greedy to want more money
- I have to work hard to get more money
- I am not good at managing money
- Getting money is hard
- My family has always been poor, and I cannot escape that
- I do not deserve to earn or receive more money
- Others need money more than me
- Having more money is selfish
- I cannot make money doing something I love
- Being happy is more important than having money
- Making money means I will not have time to spend with my family and friends
- Others will change their opinion of me if I have lots of money
- My friends and family will want me to pay for everything
- I will be wanted for my money, not for me

If any of these resonate, you must return to the Releasing Process and change your perspective.

The currency in your bank account can reflect your self-worth. Money energy is flowing to you, but you cannot accept it, which is why releasing work is important. This will change how you view yourself so you can align more fully with your abundant prosperous self; the one who knows how deserving you are. It knows how to allow and welcome opportunities and synchronicities, as well as currency and other rewards.

Definitions

Money is an energy and currency (cash in your bank account) is the manifestation of that energy. There is no end to money energy as, with all energy, it cannot be created or destroyed. It can be recycled. When you experience a lack of money, it is either because of your limiting beliefs or your lack of allowing. You are keeping the funnel, through which money energy and currency flow to you, constricted and small. What's interesting is that if you feel a lack in other areas of your life, it can also affect your allowing of currency into your experience.

As with all Energetics, this needs practice. Once you have cleared your limiting beliefs, you must check that your physical cells are also clear as you begin to adopt an abundant money mindset.

Do this by learning to see abundance in its widest sense, all around. Instead of focusing on money, look at the abundance of:

- Nature - trees, plants and animals
- Friendship and love you experience daily
- Time or talents you have, as well as opportunities

This is a daily practice so that you understand the concept of lack is false. There is no lack. If you believe, as I do, that everything is working out then when you need currency to flow to you, it will. It will not always come through your work (whether employed or self-employed). It may come through a win, gift or drawdown from an ISA, a pension or another financial product. It may be a refund or voucher.

I have been guilty of focusing on income via my paid work and, of course, it does but I have also received money as a housewarming gift, a redundancy package, and a win on a charity lottery. If you allow it, money will flow in the easiest way possible.

Imagine money energy as a large river, like the Amazon, at its widest where the water moves steadily, without hindrance. Coming off it are lots of tributaries. Some have become silted by limiting beliefs, others blocked by a refusal to allow. Some have water wheels, mills or locks which affect the flow; obstacles you place in your way and only occasionally allow currency in. Then there are the tributaries that flow easily, with no obstruction to their destination. These are easy manifestations that often occur without you even thinking about it. There is no restriction on how much you can receive, apart from your imagination and willingness to allow and align.

Depending on where you are in your money journey, this might sound fanciful. I hear you grumbling about there being no restriction. How on earth can that be true when your experience says otherwise? I am here to remind you that there is an endless supply of money energy and there can be no limit to what you allow yourself to receive, apart from the limitations you place.

How can currency arrive?

When you start thinking about the 'How?', you restrict the flow of money energy because you are limiting it to your thoughts. Most of us think of currency arriving via our work i.e. our weekly or monthly remuneration. For many, there is a cap on how much they believe they can receive that way.

Be open to the idea that money energy constantly flows to us and the 'How?' does not matter. Currency can flow to you in different ways, including the following:

- Salary: regular employment income
- Credit: loans, mortgages and credit cards
- Freelancing/side hustles: for project services rendered
- Business ventures: profits earned
- Investments: returns on e.g. shares, bonds or real estate
- Rent: from the lease of property or assets
- Royalties: intellectual property i.e. books, music or patents
- Shareholder dividends: profits distributed by a company
- Pensions: regular payments after retirement
- Social security: government payments to those eligible
- Alimony: financial support from a former spouse
- Child support: payments for the financial needs of a child
- Gifts: money received from family or friends
- Inheritance: money and assets from a person's estate
- Grants/scholarships: for education or research purposes
- Prizes/awards: money for winning competitions
- Rewards: the monetary value of presents has a currency
- Gifts: coffees, meals and other treats have a currency

- Sale of unwanted clothing or furniture: financial payments
- Cashback sites e.g. Quidco/Top Cash: earn as you purchase

You may say that loans, mortgages and credit cards are debt. They are not yours and have to be repaid. I agree, but they are a means for money energy to flow currency to you. Money energy is neutral energy and does not think in terms of credit or debt. I am not suggesting that you get into debt to fund your lifestyle. You are being shown that this amount of currency is trying to make its way into your experience and this is the simplest way to make it happen. If you are shown that this amount is available, how else can you allow yourself to receive it?

If you are struggling with repaying debt, look up the *'Snowball Debt Method'*. It suggests that you make a list of all your debts, then pay the minimum on all except your smallest debt, which you should pay off as quickly as you can. Repeat this process with each debt.

If it will help, I have a Snowball Debt Tracker in my Etsy store https://energeticsco.etsy.com which you can purchase, along with money affirmations and an income tracker.

Your actions so far:

- You have identified your money story and whether you have a poverty or abundant mindset.
- You have sought the help of your Higher Self, to release your limiting beliefs around money.
- You have realised different ways currency can flow into your experience.

It can feel challenging, so take your time with these and allow your Higher Self to guide you through the Releasing Process. Notice how your emotions ramp up and ask, "What is this feeling trying to show me? What experience does this relate to?"

By doing these three things, you have begun the process of changing your mindset and opening up your allowing. This may not show up as more currency, initially. Instead, you may receive more compliments, wake up more positive, someone may treat you to coffee or a meal, or have an idea that excites and inspires you to act.

30-day Process to open your Money Flow

This process is designed to help you open up to the abundance i.e. increase your allowing and enable your money flow, which is currently available. This can be used alongside the Releasing Process as you change your limiting beliefs, or as a standalone process. It can be repeated regularly.

Eventually, the first two steps will become automatic.

Use the next 30 days to embed the abundant mindset and begin to manifest money intentionally. You will need a journal or diary. Writing things down is important as it makes things real.

1. Create an evidence list of all the ways currency flows to you. Each day, before bed, record everything that you have received. It could be a coffee, a doughnut or a bunch of flowers. Write down the monetary value of each item. At the end of the 30 days, count the monetary value of all the gifts you received. This will show that money energy is flowing to you constantly and you need to expand your allowing.

2. Set this intention each morning:

   Today is going to be a wonderful day. I am open and ready to accept new opportunities to receive currency into my experience. I love receiving currency and currency loves me.

   This will help to open your mind to the possibility of unexpected income. Your subconscious will believe what you tell it. If you tell your mind that you are open to unexpected opportunities, it will find ways to show them to you. It will also stop the belief that you can only receive money through your job or business. That is NOT the only way.

3. Set a target for how you will spend the money. Will you repay a debt or pay a deposit for a house, car or holiday? Will you buy yourself a pair of Louboutin or a new tech you saw online? How do you set a target? Historically, you might have said, "I need to receive £3000 to pay my monthly bills." However, that target will not excite you or make you celebrate. Connect with your Higher Self and ask to be shown a figure that will bring excitement, joy and a sense of accomplishment. You can set any target you want from £1 to £1,000,000 or more.

   A word of caution: I want you to be excited about the next 30 days but, depending on your target, your energy and action must reflect that. It is possible to manifest £1,000,000 but the corresponding action must be as huge. Personally, I like to manifest incrementally. I start with how I want to spend my money. That always excites me and it is normally something to do with my family. I always check with Athaliah if it is achievable and how long it will take.

You can listen to this audio here.

**"Being Open to opportunities
and receiving Currency"**

4. Consider where to store the incoming currency so it does not get lost in your normal income and expenses. Have a specific account or storage place called your 'Manifesting Pot' or 'Bucket List Account'. This will make the manifesting process feel light and easy.

5. Notice the nudges or inspiration from your Higher Self that may be through conversations which spark a thought, or you may see something as you drive along. Notice! Notice! Notice!

Be practical

- **Know your figures:** Do you know income and expenditure? Create a spreadsheet or note these details in a book.

- **Use what you pay for:** As you check your accounts, consider if you are getting value for money and still using the products and services you are paying for.

- **Be clear on your savings:** Holidays, home maintenance and replacing your car all cost money. Consider how much you can save for these.

- **Debts:** Do you have debts to repay? Can you move credit card debts to zero per cent cards?

- **Boost your income:** Is there an easy way to boost your income e.g. changing your current account?

By knowing your figures, you will feel more in control of your money and feelings of shame will be reduced. As with everything, re-educating yourself can take a while. Be persistent and consistent.

Are you a Process Manifester or a Target Manifester?

Denise Duffield Thomas coined these terms to describe how you like to manifest. It can be helpful to know your type.

I am a Process Manifester as the process excites me and I need to experience the emotions of the outcome during the manifesting process. As I go through the month, I look for nudges and opportunities to get excited for my manifestation.

A Target Manifester is excited by the number they aim for, which keeps them on track each day as the target motivates them to act.

Now that you know the figure you want to manifest, your time-frame and your manifester type, it is time to act.

Action can be in the form of learning e.g. if selling an item, you may need to learn how to market your photos on social media. Or if your action involves investment you may need to understand ISAs or stocks and shares.

If you are a target manifester, the figure excites you. It gets you out of bed in the morning and focuses your mind. If you are a process manifester, you will enjoy the process of manifesting. I love the thrill of selling old clothes and books. I earned £100 in one month and loved every moment of it.

Below, I have given some ideas on how to act. Remember that your Higher Self will know the simplest way to receive your target, so tune in and ask.

Example:

I want to manifest £625 over the next 30 days to pay for the accommodation and flight to a retreat. I get excited about this by thinking about who I will spend time with and what we will do. Being in France generates more excitement and I will research the surrounding areas. This helps bring the feelings of the retreat into my experience now. I will look for lots of opportunities to do that.

A target manifester would break down the £625 target so that £21 each day must be manifested to meet it. By breaking it down, it seems more achievable which can motivate action.

As a process manifester, the journey excites me. As I stay motivated, imagining the conversations, and revisiting the website to look at the venue, it will excite me and encourage me to act. I may take similar actions as a target manifester but how we remain motivated is different.

Why is it important to take action?

Manifesting is not about sitting back and doing nothing. You can play an active role in your receiving. This will hone your manifesting skills and greatly increase your allowing. You prove to yourself that you are resourceful and can achieve what you are striving for. Plan to take small actions each day towards the goal.

What can you sell or rent?

- Could you create a new offering for your clients to help them achieve their transformation?

- Are there items at home that you no longer need or use that could be sold on eBay or other apps? Is there a referral link to share with friends and family? I recently earned an unexpected £5 by doing just that.

- Do you have an idea of something to sell? Perhaps sell photos to an agency that supplies bloggers or influencers. My son's friend sells his music online.

- Could you create and sell 'How to' sheets for your area of expertise via Etsy or similar? You will have to learn about hashtags and how to promote your online store but it is doable, so do not be discouraged.

- Do you have a room to rent out? It does not have to be forever, just until you have met your target. Be clear about who you want to rent to and for how long. Before starting, check your house insurance policy and complete the appropriate paperwork.

- Could you rent your driveway if you live near a station? Some schemes allow you to do this safely.

Find a referral partner

Is there anyone you could collaborate with to act as a referral partner for a small fee?

In my previous business, I offered £50 Amazon vouchers for referrals for my 3-month package, which I sold for £1500.

Essentially, the hard work was done for me, and I earned an extra £1450 for each referral.

Free money available

- Some UK banks offer up to £200 to move your account.
- Use a company that offers cashback.
- Generate points. I may apply for a credit card attached to an airline for my retreat in France.

Actions while employed full-time

- Take opportunities for overtime.
- Aim for available bonuses.
- Find out if your company has in-house incentives.
- Buy shares in your company.
- Consider a side job, such as dog-walking, washing cars at the weekend, or becoming a taxi driver.
- Open an online store.

Audit your bank accounts

Examine your expenses each month. Immediately cancel any direct debits, standing orders or subscriptions not being used. Move that money into your wish list savings pot.

Each of these small actions will lead to currency manifestation. If you feel unsure, or cannot think of anything, ask your Higher Self for the easiest action towards your goal. That step will feel good and expand your vibration. You will increasingly trust your ability to receive from your Higher Self and be more confident to act and reach your manifesting target.

What could go wrong?

Sometimes when we embark on this kind of journey, we receive an influx of bills, some unexpected. This happens because we have relaxed and exhaled. When there feels like there is a shortage of currency, it's like we hold our breath waiting for the next bill. When we receive some currency, we relax and the bills flood in.

This happened to me as I was writing this chapter. I see it as a test of my resolve. Can I hold my balance and not panic? Can I trust that there will ALWAYS be more currency flowing to me?

It is an opportunity and invitation to look at your beliefs. Do you have a latent belief that currency can only flow in when you need it, rather than just because you want it? In other words, you can only have money if there is a bill to pay.

You might feel constricted in other areas, perhaps a physical reaction e.g. constipation. Your body is a good indicator of how you are doing energetically. This is just evidence of change, that something new is happening. You are using the bills to call in more money, but you do not have to do it that way.

You could choose to call in the currency more easily but, for now, this is the most practised way for you. So, allow your desires in.

The Visceral Impact of Handling Money

We live in a digital world where money is moved around at the touch of a keypad. Some of you will have bank accounts that offer digital saving pots or spaces which work well for you. But some of you need the visceral physical experience of handling money to break money patterns and create a feeling of an excess of money that is available to you.

This can be done by having a savings box or putting money in envelopes to save for holidays, work on your home, etc. Personally, I get a huge rush each time I stuff money into my envelopes.

You can listen to this audio here.

"A Rampage of Allowing"

Finally, manifesting is meant to be fun and as my friend Sue says, "Easy peasy, light and breezy!" If you have an open-minded friend who is curious and will help you stay on track and feel positive, then do this with them. Accountability and sharing will generate excitement and motivation for you both.

Are you ready to start opening up your money flow? Yes? Let's go!

Your money journey will continue to evolve as you do. As you grow and change your money beliefs, fears or limitations may unexpectedly appear. Writing this book brought up fears for me. I know this book is needed but I feared no one would buy it. To overcome this, I had to go back to the energy flow and feel how this book will go out into the world and reach those it is meant to. As I feel this energy, my fears drop away and I can go back into the flow.

Upsizing the manifesting

Like many things in life, manifesting is a habit we can practise and perfect. I have suggested that you start small and gradually build up to bigger desires. This is partly to build your confidence and belief in your ability to manifest but also to help you be energetically in the location of your desire.

Do not try to run before you can walk. Start with small things with little emotional impact on you e.g. a parking space wherever you go. That will give you the ease to build up to someone taking you out for a coffee or a meal which will give you fun and trust. This will gradually build up to the things that you most desire.

You will have seen stories about people winning the jackpot but then, a few years later, not having any money. This is a good example of having a huge desire but not being vibrationally ready. Their vibration did not match their desire. They probably still had limiting beliefs around money, poor money hygiene and habits and, although they had millions, they still felt poor.

Remember that we live in an energetic universe. In order to match your desire vibrationally and hold onto that lottery jackpot money, you must feel rich (i.e. not feel lack in **any** area of your life)

Summary

What is your money story?

Money is linked to self-worth and allowing.

If money could talk, what would it say to you?

Poverty mindset versus abundant mindset.

Release your money-limiting beliefs.

Money can flow in many ways.

30-day process to opening your money flow.

The visceral effect of handling money.

My Love Letter to You

Dear friend,

We have come to the end of our journey in this book. We hope that as you have read it from cover to cover, you have felt excited about connecting with your beautiful glorious Higher Self; inspired to play with energy and feel empowered to have a go at creating the life you want.

So where should you start? At the beginning, by connecting to your Higher Self, who is eagerly waiting for your "Hello". This is the start of a beautiful friendship of equals and, if you allow it, will bring you comfort, laughter and a knowing that someone loves you, no matter where or who you are.

Higher Selves are a chatty bunch so be open to the signs of them reaching out to you. Your Higher Self is a unique loving extension of you, filled with knowledge and wisdom to help you enjoy life more.

The journey will not always be easy and will have a few twists and turns. In those moments, you might forget your Higher Self or that you can wield energy like a Jedi Master. Those are the moments that you go into your head. But you will remember and, when you do, it will be easier each time to slip back into a place of trust and ease.

When you do forget, do not be hard on yourself. As physical humans, we make mistakes and that is okay. It is how we learn. Remember **YOU** get to choose **YOUR** life and YOU get to choose YOUR thoughts. As my friend Jenny says, "You are the greatest influencer of your life."

This journey will continue until it is your turn to transition because your physical life is finite. Do not grieve for that. Instead, make each day as much of a celebration as you can, via your senses, and be determined to live life to the full. Know that, once you have transitioned, you will be reunited with your Higher Self, family, friends and pets who have gone before. Your life experience will be added to the knowledge of the wider collective.

But enough words.

Now is the time for you to put our words into action. Remember not to take it too seriously. Have fun, stay curious and make sure you keep a note of the changes you experience. You can repeat the processes as often as you like but stop if it becomes overwhelming or feels hard. That is a sign that you need a rest to let the energies settle.

You will return to the Releasing Process as you start deliberately manifesting your dreams. It will help you to trust that what you want is coming, as well as to trust your ability to become a successful manifester.

In writing this book, we have had a lot of fun revisiting what I have learned with Athaliah over the last five years. With the Energetics woven into it, there is no book like it. These Energetics are designed to support you on your journey, to help you to find the easiest way forward with your Higher Self and to help you have fun.

I would love to hear how your "great experiment" went and what you have learned and experienced.

thebookreport@energeticseverydaywithsunayanaclark.co.uk

Lots of love

Sunayana and Athaliah xx

Acknowledgments

The list of people I could thank is endless. If you do not see your name, please do not take offence but know that I am grateful for your energetic and physical contributions in my life.

Baba, Ma & Brinda.

Athaliah, the Higher-Self collectives and my non-physical team.

Jenny, Emily, Louise, Bryony, Sue and Karen H.

Sarah and the DOMAIN Leaders.

The Energetics Every Day Facebook Community.

The Energetics Every Day Business Support Group.

The 5DE Community.

Alyson S.

All my clients who have taught me so much over the last 25 years.

My mentors.

My editing team: Sarah, Christine and Matt.

About the author

Originally born in Kolkata India, Sunayana has spent the majority of her life in North London. In 2021, Sunayana won the best Mental Health Therapy business award in the Innovation and Excellence Awards and was quoted in Forbes Magazine.

Sunayana is a qualified Reflexologist, Usui Reiki Master Teacher, Bowen Technique Practitioner and a Free Mind Hypnotherapist. She has a successful private practice as well as worked with the clients of OAP charities, Cancer Charities and the North London Motor Neurone Disease Association in a paid and voluntary capacity helping patients to feel better.

In 2018 she switched her focus to helping individuals with anxiety. In this work she helped couples dealing with infertility problems, young people with anxiety, PTSD and depression. Sunayana does not believe that you have to live with anxiety.

Sunayana is obsessed with all things energetic and the idea of if you change the energy, then the physical reality must change too. Her work is centred on the idea of how can she empower people to live a TRULY ABUNDANT life. She talks to her Higher Self Athaliah all the time and their favourite things to do together are paint and cook.

She is married with one son and has 2 cats. She is an amateur artist, loves sci-fi films, deep conversations over delicious food and books. She is currently in the second phase of her life and loving it!

Printed in Great Britain
by Amazon

47207326R10099